ETHICS FOR THE PROFESSIONS

A Christian Perspective

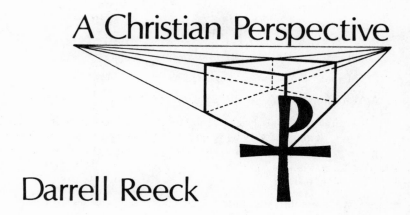

Darrell Reeck

AUGSBURG Publishing House • Minneapolis

ETHICS FOR THE PROFESSIONS

Manufactured in the United States of America

To My Parents

Contents

Acknowledgments

In addition to the permissions cited elsewhere, I am grateful for permission to reprint the following items:

The quotation from Talcott Parsons on page 29 from "Professions," reprinted from *International Encyclopedia of the Social Sciences,* David L. Sills, editor, Volume 12, page 536. Copyright © 1968, Crowell and Macmillan, Inc.

The quotation from Thomas Kelly on page 45 from *A Testament of Devotion,* copyright © 1941 by Harper and Row Publishers Inc., English edition copyright © 1957 by Hodder and Stoughton Limited.

William Law's description of love on page 46 quoted from *Instrument of Thy Peace* by Alan Paton, copyright © 1968 by The Seabury Press, Inc.

The quotation from Mila A. Aroskar on page 61, copyrighted by the American Journal of Nursing Company and reprinted from *American Journal of Nursing,* April 1980.

The quotations from the Stephen R. Graubard articles on pages 77, 84, and 85 from *Daedalus,* Journal of the American Academy of Arts and Sciences (109:1, Winter 1980), Cambridge, Mass.

The quotation from Theodore Purcell on page 98, reprinted from the *Business and Society Review,* Number 13, Spring 1975, copyright © 1975, Warren, Gorham and Lamont Inc., 210 South Street, Boston, Mass. All rights reserved.

Introduction

After some ten years of teaching a course entitled "Professional Ethics for a Technological Era," I have come to the point of wanting to set down some thoughts for the professions in the modern world, thoughts that build on religious tradition. I rebel against the tendency in modern life to split personal life from work life and to divorce work from religious perspectives. I have sketched out an understanding of both the world and religious vision that allows Christians to reaffirm their ethical heritage in the professional workplace, yet without simply imposing their own beliefs on clients, colleagues, or society. Since we are dealing with the modern world, science, technology, large organizations and bureaucracy figure prominently into the picture. And because we are examining ethics, philosophy is important also. The object, then, is to develop a basic understanding of Christian ethics that will help professionals become morally alert to their practices in the modern, pluralistic world.

Unlike many treatments of professional ethics, my approach avoids restricting the focus to one particular work discipline. The ordinary approach is to examine the ethics of medical practice or of nursing or of business management or of some other specialty. This approach has the merit of allowing an extensive treatment of problems unique to one field. However, it fails to provide professionals in the one field with orientation to other professions. Second, it tends to split the professions from each other at the expense of the development of a unified professional outlook that informs all separate disciplines. Third, it is unrealistic to expect the smaller professions to develop an extensive body of ethics literature and smaller colleges to provide a separate ethics course for each professional program. While recognizing that a general approach will not explore the issues unique to any one discipline in great depth, a general survey of professional ethics can be of great value by providing cross-fertilization among disciplines, by cultivating one general professional outlook, and by producing a text to support a general course in professional ethics. Readers who wish to pursue special problems in their own disciplines will find suitable references in the bibliographies at the end of each chapter.

The overall argument assumes a preference for an *ethic of responsibility*, which treats ethics as an art of mature judgment rather than as a scientific or formal logical application of a particular system of rules. Though favoring the ethic of responsibility, I have, however, provided a basic introduction to several forms of ethics so that readers will gain an orientation to the alternatives.

One of the features of the ethic of responsibility is very careful listening to the history and values of professions themselves to identify moral motifs native to the professional life. The procedure of listening to the professions led me to identify *enablement* as a moral theme indigenous to the professions and deeply rooted in long-standing ideals of client relationships. An open and forward-looking religious outlook is supportive of the ethic of enablement in the context of modern society. The enemy to this vision of professional ethics is the combination of the *exploitation of clients* supported by *egoism*.

The outline of the book begins with the structure of professional ethics, then moves through the contemporary setting of professional ethics to issues arising out of client, peer, superior, and governmental relations. A discussion of professional responsibility in the broader world precedes the concluding chapter. In my understanding, there are four main elements to the structure of professional ethics, and I have devoted one chapter in Part One to each of them. Chapter 1 deals with the identity of the professional, Chapter 2 with the professional organization, Chapter 3 with the art of ethics, and Chapter 4 with professional ethics codes and committees. The contemporary social setting, examined in Part Two of the book, has two chapters, one (5) devoted to science and technology and the other (6) to large organizations. Generally I begin with considerations close to the personal concerns of professionals and move toward wider circles of interest (from the professional to problems of professionals in large organizations, and from relationships with those near at hand to responsibility toward the broader world.) Part Three deals with some specific issues in professional ethics.

I must mention with gratitude my colleagues at the University of Puget Sound, particularly John Magee, Professor of Philosophy, who encouraged me to start writing and offered criticism of the first draft. Robert Waldo, Professor of Business Administration, and Jeffrey Bland, Associate Professor of Chemistry, have teamed with me in teaching the course out of which this book springs and have shaped my outlook on many points. Students, too, may recognize their mark in this book in some of the ideas expressed, particularly Peter Hapeman, who criticized the entire first draft. Anneke Mason, Jill Sharrard, and Julie Boyle typed drafts, and the Trustees' Enrichment Fund provided financial assistance. To these and to many more persons and groups, I express my sincere thanks while assuming responsibility for any errors still remaining.

PART ONE

STRUCTURE
OF
PROFESSIONAL ETHICS

ONE

The Professional
and the Imperative of Moral Choice

The imperative of moral choice is built into the very nature of professionalism. Chapter 1 introduces the first of the four basic components of the structure of professional ethics. *The structure of professional ethics is the ensemble of moral skills, institutional mandates, and psychological identities that inevitably influence a professional's reflection on the ethical dimensions of problems encountered in one's practice.* The first component of this structure is the nature of the professional.

WHAT IS A PROFESSIONAL?

Bill Murphy's biography, in which he explores a profession and trains for it, portrays some of the modern meanings of the term *professional:*

Bill Murphy is a physical therapist. He set his course toward this profession several years ago when a number of things became clear to him. First, he realized that he was happiest when he was helping others. Second, he did extremely well in sciences. He began to lean toward a medical career and got a summer job in a hospital as an aide. In this setting Bill learned about the great variety of medical professions and occupations. He saw doctors, of course, but also he became aware of technicians, pharmacists, physical and occupational therapists, and many others. Bill final-

15

ly opted for physical therapy for a variety of reasons: he liked the work setting, the patient interaction, and the morale of the therapists he knew. He also believed that he could successfully master the relatively rigorous training. He learned that both training and work would probably be available. As his college years progressed, he was somewhat surprised to be required to take courses in a wide variety of subjects, not just sciences and physical therapy. "The therapist is broadly educated as well as technically competent," his faculty advisor told him. Finally he graduated, completed his residency, won a state license to practice, and was accepted as a member of the American Physical Therapy Association.

Bill's case, which like many others in this book is a true-to-life but composite portrait, brings to light some connotations of the term *professional*. As used today, it means "a person who is trained and certified in a recognized body of skills, uses them in treating the needs of clients, and is obliged to standardized levels of competence and ethics generated by the profession and acknowledged by the public." A professional, in other words, is simply a highly trained member of the work force with certain characteristics of training and discipline that more or less set him or her off from other categories of workers.

"Well, then, how about my automobile mechanic?" someone might ask. "He seems to meet the same criteria as Bill." It is true that some technical workers have committed themselves to ethical practices developed by their associations, in addition to being highly trained. But they still may not be professionals in the sense in which we are using the term. Our more restricted meaning implies knowledge of history, society, culture, and the arts, as well as basic intellectual skills of communication and logic. American higher education conforms to this pattern by requiring a liberal arts education prior to or along with special professional training. A professional must be able to diagnose and to prescribe in wholes—whole persons, systems, societies, or even environments. That explains why Bill found himself in liberal arts as well as in technical courses. In addition, membership in a professional body is expected. The professional body determines the standards of practice to which the individual is held accountable.

A more general meaning than we have in mind is conveyed when a person says, "I am a professional at . . . , " and then adds teaching, accounting, carpentry, or criminal investigation. For instance, a woman said, "A woman who truly devotes herself to homemaking can be a true professional." What one conveys by using the term this way has less to do with a type of training and discipline than with a basic commitment to, and high degree of skill in, one's particular way of making a living and of contributing to society, whatever that may be. This more general meaning of *profession* can apply to workers in virtually any field and its use suggests that a professional in the more restricted sense shares much in common with workers in other categories of labor. By no means is the difference between the restricted and the general uses of the term without overlap. The restricted sense actually roots in and grows out of the general sense. This constitutes an important point for the meaning of professional work, a point we'll develop later when we touch upon it in discussing the idea of *vocation*. Here the point is to acknowledge that our mechanic could be professional in the general sense, even though the narrower one occupies our main interest.

Another concept will help to provoke some important ideas for the definition that we will shortly formulate. Robert L. Herrick, a sociologist, has written that professionals ought to be understood as persons who have "guilty knowledge," or knowledge of things "dangerous" to know. The surgeon, for instance, has "guilty knowledge" because he can remove an organ from a living body, and the priest has "guilty knowledge" because he can determine God's will. The psychological therapist can shape the human mind, and the result of a decision by a business manager may be the employment of hundreds in useful jobs or their unemployment. All such forms of knowledge are "dangerous."

Knowledge of such things is necessary for the continuation of human society, even though it normally entails "guilt." Professionals are those workers whom society has commissioned to deal in "guilty knowledge." They are ones whose decisions potentially have enormous, even frightful, impact on other human beings and on the environment. Because of the dangers connected with their work, professionals are expected to undergo highly controlled training and to adhere to high ethical standards (Herrick, 1978).

The basic point made by Herrick is that a professional is entrusted with the making of decisions with potentially dangerous consequences on behalf of less knowledgeable, and therefore more defenseless, clients who will be affected for better or worse by the adequacy of the decision. Even though we will not adopt the term "guilty," since it raises many questions that would divert us from the main concern, its use by Herrick forcefully drives home the point that professionals are set off from other workers by particularly heavy responsibilities. Even though there is no absolute difference between professionals and other workers, trying to distinguish between them is not merely an academic exercise. Rather it is an attempt to point out the relatively higher responsibility borne by professionals for the welfare of others.

Summarizing, we may now define a *professional* in the restricted contemporary sense as: *(1) a broadly educated person, (2) possessing highly developed skills and knowledge, (3) working under the discipline of an ethic developed and enforced by a body of peers, and (4) commissioned to satisfy complex needs by making judgments entailing potentially dangerous consequences.* Bill seems to qualify for consideration under this definition, whereas the mechanic and many other classifications of skilled workers do not.

Three brief parting comments on this definition are required. In the first place it assumes a secularized understanding of the term *professional*. Later we shall learn that that concept can be understood helpfully from a religious perspective as well. In the second place this definition does not necessarily embody a *constructive* ethical thrust. An ethic is stipulated, but the content of that ethic is not suggested. A perverse professional ethic, like that of the Nazi staffs, is not ruled out by definition. We shall work toward a definition of the term *professional* with a positive moral content (see Chapter 3). But third, the definition does make it clear that ethical choice is a built-in feature of professional work. Without ethics no one can be professional in the full meaning of the term, regardless of the number of clients she treats or the complexity of the problems he solves.

WHAT IS PROFESSIONAL ETHICS? — AN OVERVIEW

Lois, a C.P.A., felt unable, at a certain point in her career, to do full justice to keeping up with both new developments in her field and also to general reading necessary to keep abreast of important social trends. Although she understood both of these to be obligations, she had only a very limited amount of time for reading.

To be most fully professional, which alternative should she choose? Or should she cut down on time devoted to family, friends, or church? Each alternative has ethical implications.

Dr. Mabel Silver labored in general practice in a small town deep in the steaming West African forest. She felt it her obligation to treat as many ill as possible since no other medical care was available for many miles. She asked of her patients only whether they needed treatment, not whether they could pay. She developed procedures allowing her to personally treat up to 100 people per hour in her outpatient clinic.

Would this missionary physician have been more professional had she chosen to limit the number of patients, giving her more time to give perhaps better care to just a few? How would she determine which few to treat?

To resolve dilemmas like these, in which neither alternative seems obviously right, one must be able to weigh the shades of right and wrong, better and worse. Ethics is an *imperative* for the professional, not a luxury.

Here we shall explore some initial meanings of *ethics*, both in general and as applied to the issues characteristically faced by the professions. *Ethics is the art of reflection on the moral meaning of human action.*[1] *Action,* an important term in this definition, has a broad scope. It includes what individuals and groups do to each other, to others, and to their environment. An adequate ethical understanding of action likewise requires a knowledge of the circumstances, including the motives and values, that give rise to them.

---

1. This definition is based on McCoy, *et. al.,* 1975.

Another important concept is the notion of *moral*. A great share of human action has moral significance. This becomes apparent when one raises standards for action, such as the justice or injustice of a judge's decision, the truth or falsity of a physician's prognosis, or the good or bad consequences of a corporate business policy. To do ethics, then, is to apply one's intelligence to human action using standards of moral evaluation.

Having just introduced ethics in general we want, second, to explore professional ethics as a particular facet of the broader topic. *Professional ethics is the application of standards of moral evaluation to the significant problems of professional life*. It is reflection on the moral meaning of professional action. This being the case, everyone who would do professional ethics must know something about both the practices and procedures generally favored in ethical reflection and also be able to apply them to the problems of the professions. While there is no one ethic that all professionals should utilize, the ability to apply systematically one fitting approach to a spectrum of issues is essential to the professional.

Ethics involves both personal and social considerations, small-scale and large-scale dimensions. Those familiar with the distinction between micro- and macro-economics may find the analogy helpful. It is regrettable that much of the moral reflection about the problems of professionals today is limited to personal ethics, or to issues relevant only to individual choices and motives. It is, of course, just as possible for organizations as for individuals to serve as enablers or to act as exploiters. To concentrate solely on personal ethics is to overlook the great moral significance of institutions.

To clarify the difference between social and personal ethics, let us consider the following example:

An automobile parks in front of the office of a woodworking firm and a suited, slender woman carrying a briefcase gets out. The tag on her case identifies her as Lois Carlton, C.P.A. Before she enters the office, she pauses. She needs to reflect on how to introduce a certain decision she had previously made to her client, the president of the firm. In undertaking the firm's final audit it had become clear to her that she could obtain two substantially different net profit figures depending on which method of accounting she would choose to apply. The more conservative method would produce a lower profit figure. She knew that this decision was a matter of special interest to the owner of the woodworking firm because he intended to sell the business during the coming year. For some time Lois had been in a quandary. She was well aware that she could lose the account if the president were displeased with her work. On the other hand, she believed that the proper course from the point of view of her own principles, as well as those of her profession, would probably be to choose the conservative method. She made her choice. Her remaining problem now was to make the decision as palatable to the president as possible.

Lois' quandary illustrates a personal ethical decision of the sort that professionals frequently face. Other examples abound. For instance, in the medical field the owner of a private clinic may have to answer: would it be better to terminate a patient's therapy when he can no longer pay or to continue with the needed treatment even though the loss of his revenue would strain the finances of the clinic?

Now, in contrast, consider a social-ethical situation:

The American Institute of Architects has been concerned with an immense redefinition of design standards for new construction with a view toward making this nation more energy-efficient. A series of high-level committees has been hard at work developing new design protocols for adoption by the A.I.A. Ultimately the entire professional association will have to change its way of thinking on such matters as energy recapture and energy loss.

Social ethics applies when the values at stake involve an entire organization or institution, as in this case, the retooling of an entire professional protocol toward the goal of conservation.

Looking back at Lois Carlton, one can also detect a social-ethical aspect of her situation. It has to do with the creation and maintenance of the professional codes governing accounting practices. The C.P.A. code, for instance, encourages the more conservative approach. The rule guides the individual C.P.A. in making her decision and gives her a strong supporting rationale in representing it to the client. Morally the code is significant: it helps to protect anyone with an interest in the woodworking firm by giving a more accurate picture of its financial strength.

To summarize, *social ethics is reflection upon the moral significance of the action of institutions and organizations*. It is as important as personal ethics, which is *reflection upon the moral significance of the action of individuals in primary relationships*, yet it has generally been given less attention. To compensate for this neglect, we shall devote more attention in the following pages to *social* than to *personal* ethics.

How is morality different from ethics? This is a question often asked. *Morality consists of socially approved patterns and norms of proper conduct*. Morality shades over into ethics when systematic reflection begins to occur. Maxims, such as that children should obey their teachers and citizens, the law, are examples of morality. We do ethics when we debate why children should obey their teachers and whether citizens are obligated to obey all laws or only good laws. Morality is pre-ethical; it exists prior to systematic, questioning thought on the issues.

Morality and ethics are closely related to the way one views reality as a whole. Anthropologists and historians have confirmed this through studies of diverse cultures. *"Worldview" is the framework of one's thinking that sets out the way one holds reality actually and fundamentally to be.*[1] Just as one's worldview always implies something about how one ought to act, so any given plan for action in turn reflects upon one's worldview. That is, ethics and worldviews are logically related to each other. Figure 1 provides a sketch of the relationships between ethics and worldviews.

Many, if not most, worldviews could be termed religious. That is, they embody ideas about fundamental reality such as the supernatural, human nature, the environment, and space and time, and the believers hold to these conceptions with an emotional certainty or commitment. Religion provides a powerful orientation to realities visible and invisible. This being the case, one could logically expect the world's great religions to be consulted as sources of guidance by professions and professionals. On the face of it, it would seem sensible for a Muslim, Jewish, Hindu, Buddhist, or Christian professional to expect guidance for reflection on ethical issues from his or her faith. Even organized profes-

---

1. The German, *Weltanschauung,* is richer than the English term *worldview*. It means, "looking out upon the world."

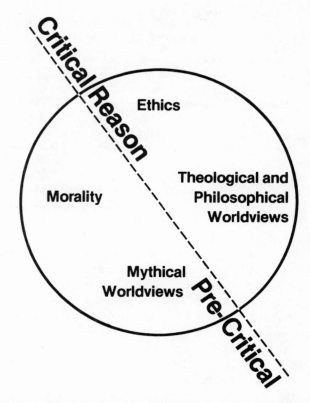

Figure 1. Illustration of the relationships between Morality and Mythical Worldviews, lying on the pre-reflective or lower-left side of the line of critical reason, and Ethics and Theological and Philosophical Worldviews, lying on the reflective or upper right side.

sional associations should be able to find ethical guidance in the religious heritage of mankind.

Yet professional associations and ethical review boards rarely, at least in the U.S. in this century, draw for guidance upon the traditions of religion to which they have easy access. Like good children of the Enlightenment, they have become secular-

ized, at least in their public deliberations and statements. A
secular humanism seems firmly lodged in place as the leading
source of guidance at the official level of professional ethics.

Nevertheless, many managers, therapists, teachers, and other
professionals as individuals may derive basic orientation from
their religious faith for their professional ethics.

> Students in an intensive course in business ethics had the oppor-
> tunity to interview several guest lecturers in significant manage-
> ment positions. The students wanted to learn what reasons these
> managers would give for advocating ethical behavior in busi-
> ness. Not just their first, superficial reasons, but their bedrock
> motives. Each speaker, when pursued far enough, ultimately fell
> back on religious teachings as the final, self-evident reason for
> ethical behavior.

In the light of these remarks it seems reasonable that we should
consider very seriously the religious dimensions of professional
ethics, both individual and social. But we cannot venture into
this complex field without some very serious reservations, recognizing that many ethical thinkers would prefer to stay clear
of the entire subject. Caution is in order for several reasons.
First, it takes only a casual observer to see that religions themselves have frequently led individuals and organizations into
disastrous policies. Hitler himself, after all, could be regarded
as a religious man. Second, religious thinkers have not exhaust-
ively thought through the application of religious ethics to the
characteristic problems of the professions. Third, some secular
humanists espouse forms of professional ethics that seem better
and more justifiable than those of many religious persons. Despite these cautionary notes, we shall attempt to move beyond
the gap between the religious heritage and professional ethics
by asking what guidance professions and professionals might
acquire from the more thoughtful representatives of religious
ethics, especially of the Judaeo-Christian tradition.

THE PROFESSIONAL —
ENABLER OR EXPLOITER?

Throughout all time professionals have been regarded by the
public, as well as by themselves, as servants of their clients'

needs and interests. Our remarks in this first chapter have echoed that ancient theme by defining the professional as one who is skilled in satisfying complex needs. The ideology of professionalism is one of client service.

A realistic view of the history of professionals, however, compels us to admit that professionals may lapse into exploitative relationships and have often done so. The occurrence of a gap between the stated goal of service and the reality of exploitation is clearly of prime importance to ethics and one to be faced with eyes open. If the mystique of service is a mask over reality, it must be stripped away.

Certainly the most extreme, and therefore perhaps the most challenging, case of professional exploitation is the participation of legal, medical, and management professionals in the Nazi enslavement and slaughter of the Jews during World War II. The Holocaust will direct our attention to important issues in professional behavior.

Hitler and the National Socialists swept to power in Germany in 1933. Their gaining office was made possible in part by support from bankers and industrial managers, two groups included in this book's concept of *professional*. By 1939 Hitler had plunged the German nation and all of Europe into World War II, and cooperating professionals fell into unparalleled depths of exploitative behavior.

The depths of the depths may well have been reached at the infamous labor and death camps at Auschwitz, Poland. Here Jewish and other prisoners were systematically worked to death under the most rationally planned and controlled conditions. The goal was to exact the greatest output of labor for the smallest input of food, clothing, and services. A systematic plan was devised for squeezing the last drop of blood. Between 3,000,000 and 5,000,000 persons perished at Auschwitz in the death and forced-labor camps during the Nazi era.

For our purposes, even more poignant than the sheer magnitude of the slaughter is the fact that professionals were largely responsible for the planning of the atrocity. The agents of death were not simply Nazi thugs. Management professionals were involved through the I. G. Auschwitz Company, a subsidiary of the I. G. Farben Corporation. Medical professionals examined and classified prisoners, selecting those for work in particular occupations. They helped to determine the maximum output obtainable at the least expense.

In the same place and elsewhere, inhuman and murderous medical experiments were conducted. Renowned medical scientists, lawyers, and industrialists were collaborators in the planning and implementation. In just one such episode, an example of a far greater epidemic of exploitation, 112 Jews were selected for completing a skeleton museum at the University of Strasbourg. They were meticulously examined; statistics on their physical characteristics were duly recorded; they were killed; more studies were conducted; and the bodies were sent to Strasbourg for defleshing.

Significantly, not all professionals cooperated with the Nazis. Some, both Jews and Gentiles, were able to flee. Others stayed in Germany but resisted Nazism mentally. A few actively engaged in resistance and even in attempts to overthrow the regime. The refusal of some professionals to cooperate with Hitler is part of the story that must not be forgotten when recounting the great depths to which others fell during the Holocaust.

One significance of Auschwitz for professional ethics is that professionals could justify their participation to themselves, regardless of how abominable their activities seemed to others. Furthermore, if one had met these managers, doctors, nurses, and lawyers in their private lives, most would have seemed like normal, middle-class, educated bourgeoisie, devoted to their families and leading exemplary lives. But the professional mystique of benevolence and service did not prevent them from employing their skills in the most intensive scheme of exploitation in Western history. Their professional moral standards did not set off the internal warning system known as *conscience*. They had an enormous blind spot that occluded their perception of the evil consequences of their deeds. They did not judge themselves to be violating standards of human dignity. At Auschwitz professional ethics totally failed to keep professional practitioners from using their skills to do evil.

Nevertheless, some redemption of professional ethics has resulted from the Holocaust. First, persons in the professional and lay worlds have come to recognize the depths to which professionals can fall and have become more alert to potential abuses of professional power. Second, other professionals were involved in defeating the scheme and in trying the criminals. Third, the Nuremburg Code, which set standards that are still followed today, was written by professionals shortly after World War II and based on the Holocaust experience. Fourth, professional ethics codes have been improved as a result of disclosures at the Nuremburg trials. Hence, another significance of the Holocaust for professional ethics has been that some reform and renewal of the true spirit of the professions was achieved.

But whatever of a positive nature resulted, the overall import of the Holocaust for the professions has been catastrophic. It has taught us to be disillusioned of the mystique that professionals are necessarily benign providers of services. Professionals may well be enablers, to be sure. But they have been proven capable of exploitation as well. Even American society in the past decade has given the world a powerful example of professional corruptability in the Watergate episode of the 1970s. And it seems likely that many preprofessionals are at present motivated toward that kind of work more from reasons of employment security than from a desire to serve. A wise professional examines his own practices and attitudes to ensure that exploitative tendencies are controlled.[1]

CONCLUSION

The ideas that we have explored lead inevitably to the conclusion that each professional acts out a morality. Simply the sheer complexity of problems professionals are asked to face dictates that their work will have profound moral significance. Moral choice is imperative for the professional, and a reasonable goal is to achieve sufficient levels of reflectiveness to raise accustomed morality to the level of critical ethics. The ideology of professionalism may lead one unwittingly into moral naivete by fostering the illusion of the good as an *a priori* of professional life. A study of professional lives, especially under Nazism, shows that this illusion needs to be stripped away. History amply demonstrates that professionals are capable of moral evil.

To be morally alert has become especially difficult due to a sep-

1. The account of the Holocaust is based on Taylor, 1949; Rubenstein, 1978; and Hilberg, 1961.

aration that has crept in between work life and the traditional sources of ethical guidance. The separation between the religious heritage and professional life is much more complete at the level of professional organizations than at that of individual lives. This suggests that we devote considerable attention to the professional organization in modern society, the problem of our next chapter and the second component in the framework of professional ethics.

References and Suggestions for Further Reading

Herrick, Robert L. 1978. "Comments and Discussion: Further Remarks on Professionalism," *Business and Professional Ethics* I (4): p. 2.

Hilberg, R. 1961. *The Destruction of the European Jews.* New York: Harper and Row, Publishers.

McCoy, Charles S., Mark Juergensmeyer, and Fred Twining. 1975. "Ethics in the Corporate Policy Process." Berkeley: Center for Ethics and Social Policy.

Rubenstein, Richard L. 1978. *The Cunning of History: The Holocaust and the American Future.* New York: Harper and Row, Colophon ed. See especially Chapter 4 for remarks on professionals and the Holocaust.

Taylor, T. 1949. "Final Report to the Secretary of the Army on the Nuremburg War Crimes Under Control Council Law No. 10." Washington, D.C.: U.S. Government Printing Office.

Think More About It

1. Ask a professional you know whether professionals always act in the client's interest. Also ask for examples in which professionals seem to have exploited the client for the professionals' own purposes or interests. You may get some surprising results.

2. Is there a significant difference between a professional and any other skilled worker such as a repairer of office machines? In what ways is the distinction breaking down?

3. Can you think of any examples in American history in which professionals fell into exploitative patterns in any way resembling those of the Holocaust?

TWO

Professional Organizations – Social Servants or Mere Monopolies?

Our focus shifts now from the individual professional and comes to rest on one of the most significant occupational organizations of our era: the profession. Renowned social scientist Talcott Parsons (1968, p. 536) holds that, "The development and increasing strategic importance of the professions probably constitute the most important change that has occurred in the occupational system of modern societies."

To many observers it appears that professions have developed into little more than bands for the protection of the self-interest of their members. David Kotelchuck (1976, p. 202) came to such a conclusion about medical professions:

> Professionalism has been the customary means by which health workers have attempted to protect their interests.

Is service to society the fundamental purpose of the profession, or is it monopoly privilege? To propose an answer, in even a tentative form, we shall obviously have to go far beyond reading what professions say about their own purposes to glimpse something of how they actually function in society and have functioned in the past. Our goal is to derive from their own history an ethical theme valid for professions.

PROFESSION DEFINED

First, what is a *profession?* The following definition parallels
that of *professional* given in Chapter 1:

> A profession is an occupational group which specializes in the
> performance of such highly developed skills for the meeting of
> complex human needs that the right use of them is achieved
> only under the discipline of an ethic developed and enforced by
> peers and by mastery of a broader contextual knowledge of the
> nature of the human being, society, the natural world, and his-
> torical trends.

A profession normally maintains an organization to ensure or
certify essential competencies. The requirement of formal knowledge implies a very close connection between the professions and
higher education as the chief institution for the development and
transmission of professional knowledge.

In sharpening our understanding of professions, and especially
of their role as vehicles of ethics, it is useful to focus on them as
subcultures.

> Two professors of history, one from the Netherlands and one
> from Canada, met for the first time traveling on a cog railway
> in Switzerland. As they talked, they found that they had com-
> mon interests, similar values, and some identical ways of look-
> ing at things, despite the differences in their national back-
> grounds. They felt at home with each other, almost like mem-
> bers of the same African tribe when they meet by chance on an-
> other continent or devotees of the same religious cult when they
> meet out in the world.

A profession develops a partial culture of its own which it culti-
vates and perpetuates within the broader society. Considered as
a subculture, a profession develops distinctive symbols, meanings, and values to orient its members to their work. That is why
a unique empathy flows between persons who have been shaped
by the same profession.

This cultural aspect of a profession plays a very crucial role
in ethics. Professional ethics is an aspect of the culture of the
professions themselves. This characteristic will make it possible
to derive the basic ethical themes of the professions from a study

of the history of the professions themselves, a task to which we shall turn after briefly assessing whether business management can be considered a profession within our definition.

IS BUSINESS MANAGEMENT A PROFESSION?

Even with a clear definition, disputes still occur over whether certain disciplines of work are professions. Almost all lists of professions include three classical ones: medicine, law, and theology. Frequently university teachers are included as a fourth. From this point on, it is no more possible to know through consensus whether a certain group is a profession than to know whether the dot in the sky is a bird, a plane, or Superman. The problem is compounded because the drive to be considered *professional* seems as widely shared in America as the belief in progress. Groups from cosmeticians to morticians to politicians wish to share in the assumed honors. Where, and how, do we draw the line?

A promising approach is to follow the lead of sociologist Wilbert E. Moore in arranging various groups at points along a scale of professionalism, ranging from more to less professional. The result is a structured understanding of the professions. At one end of the scale will be the classical professions; toward the other will be the more marginal fields such as chemistry, engineering, and therapy. A judgment about the placement of the professions on this continuum is made by applying the criteria of highly developed skills for meeting complex needs and mastery of broader contextual knowledge (Cf. Moore, 1970, pp. 4-5).

Is business management a profession, properly regarded? Since we wish to include business in our consideration of professional ethics, we must attend to this debatable issue. The debate has been going on for about a century and was forcefully joined by Emile Durkheim, a father of modern sociology. He argued against considering business as a profession on the grounds that no professional business organization existed and, more crucially, that no mechanism for ethical discipline was maintained by business persons as peers. In addition to the basic position stated by Durkheim, moreover, one meets business managers at various levels of responsibility today who do not think of themselves as professionals, nor do they care to (Durkheim, 1958, pp. 9-11, and Soble, 1978, pp. 9-10).

Others assert that business is a profession, lacking only an organization comparable to the American Medical Association or the American Institute of Architects. This point was made recently by American business leader W. M. Blumenthal. Another leader, Robert Cushman (1975, pp. 49-52), a corporate executive, recently proposed an industry-wide committee to monitor and enforce business ethics. In addition, one learns that some business managers do regard themselves as professionals. And as an important final note, the widespread acceptance of the M.B.A. as a qualifying degree and the intention of the leading management schools to make this a fully professional degree argue for thinking of business management as a profession.

How shall we resolve this dispute? Does this work discipline utilize highly developed skills for meeting complex needs? Are these skills such that the right use of them requires attention to broader contextual issues such as human nature, the nature of society, and the environment? At mid and higher levels, yes. For instance, the managers of large corporations hold important power. Within certain levels of constraint they can make decisions with highly significant consequences—positive or negative—for persons, societies, and natural environments in their range of influence. In some cases their reach extends across continents. Much the same point can be made about key decision-makers and planners in businesses of even small size. On the other hand, this work discipline still lacks effective professional organization. So, although business management cannot be strictly classified as a profession, it clearly has many professional qualities.

In summary, we may regard business management as a marginal or emerging profession, a work discipline in the process of becoming professionalized. The benefit of such an approach will come through insights derived in interprofessional dialogue and cross-fertilization. The more typical professions of medicine, law, and education stand to gain much from the pragmatism of business management, and business can gain at least as much from the long experience of others as it seeks to put its own house in order.

PROFESSIONS IN SIMPLER SOCIETIES

The rudimentary roots of our contemporary professions exist in basic human needs and values. Physical, social, and spiritual health have always been human values, and specialists in promoting them have long existed. Primitive society has had its healers, who treat illness through religious skills and herbalism. Traditional chiefs may function not only as public administrators but also as judges and perhaps as the highest official priests. Healers and chiefs are *prototypical professionals*.

Several features set the prototypical professions apart from our modern versions. For one thing, the traditionalists were unspecialized: the African healers, for instance, employed religious, magical, and technological means without distinction. For another, the traditional professions often perpetuated themselves by a system of inheritance, rather than solely by achievement through formal education and examination. But, like their modern counterparts, the traditionalists met basic human needs through the use of their special skills.

Scriptures have provided descriptions of professions in a somewhat more developed state and assist us in our quest for appropriate moral themes. Jews, Christians, and Muslims, in particular, are influenced by traditions about professions going back to at least the first millenium B.C. A class of religious professionals developed in early Israel; these priests and prophets became supreme authorities in law and religion and also performed medical functions. The commercial and bureaucratic "professionals" were the rich men and women dwelling in lavish homes on the view lots above the ancient city; Amos, the prophet, castigated them for crushing the poor in the dust by exacting exorbitant prices and rents. The prophets aid us in seeing professions at their moral best through their sensitivity to the abuse of the privileges of skill and position.

By the time of Jesus, various professions had become somewhat more specialized. He knew priests, teachers, lawyers, and physicians, as well as professional soldiers. Jesus generally denounced the legal and clerical professions with colorful and pointed imagery. He regarded them as hypocritical and legalistic. On the other hand, Jesus himself belonged to the teaching profession. He was a recognized rabbi in Galilee, a master

(almost in the contemporary British sense) with his student
disciples. And Paul had his "beloved physician," Luke, the
writer of one of the Gospels and the book of Acts. Undoubtedly,
modern attitudes toward various professions have been shaped
by the fact that generation upon generation has read the Bible,
which praises those perceived as servants of the people and
denounces those seen as exploiters.

Throughout the medieval period, particularly in Northern
Europe, the development of the professions remained relatively
rudimentary. The clergy, the primary professional group,
through its control of education, was able to set rules governing
the practice of other professions, including medicine, law, teaching, and business. There were disbenefits, but also some benefits,
to church control. Professional practice was set, at least in principle, within a coherent framework of shared values and beliefs.
Where exploitation of clients occurred, it was because the ideal
was not met, not because an ideal did not exist.

The complexity of the history of the professions is suggested
by the fact that during and even after the medieval period, occupations that we now recognize as professions were organized
as guilds. Guilds also existed for many technical and commercial
groups of workers. Standards were maintained, recruits trained,
and deviants disciplined. After the Industrial Revolution many
guilds evolved into professions.

A very important foundation for the modern professions was
laid in the sixteenth century, at the turning point between the
medieval and early modern eras, by two religious reformers,
Martin Luther and John Calvin. Though they were primarily interested in the church and its beliefs, their changes were destined
to influence all of society.

Luther's contribution to the development of professions was to
extend the concept of a "divine calling" to every worthwhile kind
of work. During the medieval period the "calling" *(vocatio)* had
been reserved for those who were chosen to enter the spiritually
superior life of the monastery. In that way of thinking, only the
religious professions were regarded as specially dignified by a
divine calling. Even today the old use of the term still lingers
when people say of one who enters the priesthood that he has a
vocation. In contrast, Luther boldly generalized this concept to

all forms of work. To him, the butcher, the baker, and not merely the priest, had a divine calling of service in the world. Luther laid the foundation for regarding every profession, as well as every other legitimate form of work, as service to God and humankind.

Calvin's contribution was to free people from following in their fathers' occupations, thus changing the main criterion for admittance to a profession from inheritance to achievement. While Luther dignified every line of work, he also limited persons to work in the same occupation as one's forebears; one was called to stay faithfully in one's place. This amounted to a vote of confidence in the static medieval social order. Calvin taught that one's calling was to serve God and people to the best of one's ability in whichever line of work one was best suited for. Freed from a certain occupation by accident of birth, an individual could now move from one niche to another in pursuit of a life of service. Every occupation could be understood as an arena for following one's calling.

In terms of the themes we are following, the Judaeo-Christian culture from Biblical times through the Reformation imbued the concept of *profession* with the moral principle of service grounded in a religious vision of God working together with people for the improvement of all creation. The doctrine of the *vocation* or *calling* became the religious and moral theme that most illuminated the meaning of the professions and of professional work.

PROFESSIONS IN MODERN SOCIETIES

Though they experienced new vitality in the centuries after 1500, the professions tended to remain small and exclusive. They had high social status because they were attached to the king and court. The needs of common people were not necessarily well served or were rather served by subprofessions such as apothecaries. Professions allowed their members to lead the "good life," the life of the leisurely gentleman, a life of refinement shielded from laborious work. This distinguished them from trade and subprofessional groups, which undertook physical labor. The professions remained clearly associated with the nobility and upper-middle classes.

As late as the eighteenth century in England and America the technical education and competence of the professions was lamentable. Physicians, for example, learned the Latin and Greek classics but had little knowledge of empirical science or even of sick patients—except through books. Physicians depended upon their stately bearing and their patients' ignorance to develop a clientele. Training for lawyers had actually deteriorated since medieval times. The most common defense of the professions was that they admitted only men of necessary social standing. They continued to serve primarily the gentry. The dynamic ideas of Calvin had, as yet, little impact on actual performance.

The Industrial Revolution brought great population growth and urbanization in Europe after 1800, radically altering the social environment in which professions functioned. Subprofessions (druggists, barristers, and surgeons), organized into guilds, continued to meet the needs of the growing urban masses for increased services. During the nineteenth century they evolved into professions while the classic professions changed from status groups into productive work groups. Professional organizations emerged clearly about midcentury, and in England were found lobbying Parliament on behalf of the interests of their members.

In America, as might be expected, the rather different social situation in which the emerging professions were set created a somewhat different history. Just as in Europe and England, higher education became a primary vehicle for the development and transmission of professional values, technical skills, and associated attitudes. But lacking a nobility or a true landed gentry, the professions were attached to the middle class and offered an avenue of expression and an arena of achievement for young men (See Elliott, 1972, pp. 14-52, and Bledstein, 1976, pp. 6-7, 121, 214-215).

In contemporary America the professions have come to represent not only a body of concentrated skill but also of wealth relative to the rest of the population, giving some weight to the suspicion raised earlier that they have become monopolies designed to protect the self-interest of their members, especially their income and job security. What additional evidence exists to support such charges? In 1978 the average personal earnings of individuals in nine professional groups from a representative list of sixteen would have ranked higher than those of laborers in strong unions, ranging from $19,030 for social scientists to $36,187 for health practitioners. Also, some groups formerly serving professional interests in the strict sense had converted partially to collective wage-negotiating agents, such as the National Education Association and its many state and local affiliates and the American Association of University Professors. In some cities and states physicians' unions had formed, and one such unit had actually been reported as having gone on strike. Local nursing association strikes and teacher strikes had become commonplace. These facts seem to lend support to the suspicions.

On the other hand, in 1978 some seven major professions were earning less than the median of personal wages paid to workers in strong unions, with clergy at the bottom of the scale. In addition, despite pay raises gained over a decade from 1967 to 1978, most professional groups were falling behind in the race with inflation. Finally, even among the most unionized of the professional groups the traditional purposes of client service were still being affirmed.

Another factor is the rapid numerical growth of professions in the present century. The sheer number of professional associations, as well as the proportion of professionals in relation to the total population, has substantially increased.

The growth of the professions varies from one society to another. In the U.S., whereas professionals accounted for some 4% of the labor force in 1900, by 1950 they accounted for 8%, and in 1966 for 13% (Moore, 1970, p. 231). The more mature economy of Sweden supported an even higher proportion of professionals relative to the total population than the U.S. Less industrialized nations have proportionately smaller professional communities, but even here the relative size of the professional sector is steadily increasing (See Figure 2).

The growth of the professions has made them more visible, more powerful, and more critical for the development of social policy. Persons concerned with social policy are correct in paying more attention to them than previously. However, growing power in itself does not substantiate the charge that professions exploit their clients. The issue centers on what is done with that power.

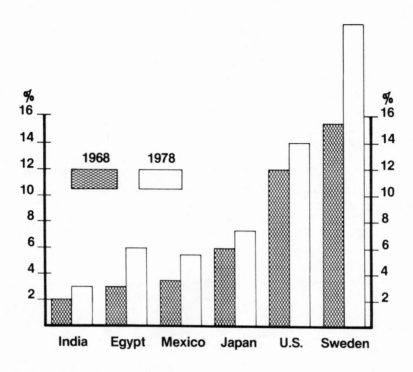

Figure 2. Table showing the percentage in total population of professional and technical workers in selected countries,1968 and 1978. Source: Yearbook of Labour Statistics (Geneva: International Labour Office, 1978).

CONCLUSION

Drawing together the themes that have emerged from this brief survey of the history of the professions, we can identify an ethical principle for professional life. An ideal that seems common to the moral heritage of the professions is that of *enablement,* which is understood as *the devotion of professional skills to meeting the needs of client groups and, ultimately, to the common good.* This is a moral value that is structured into professional groups and which they seem to impress on their constituents, as well as the public, as their main purpose. It is a principle which has roots in the religious culture with which professions have been in contact but which has been accepted as appropriate to the very notion of the profession as it has come to be understood.

In contrast to *enablement* is the theme of *exploitation,* which is the *protection and enhancement of the economic standing and other privileges of the members of the professional organization at the expense of consumer groups, clients, and the society at large.* From our short survey it is not clear that exploitation has become as central to the professions as Kotelchuck and others have claimed. Rather, professions seem to have long histories of morally ambiguous behavior. Even today, they appear neither as simply *evil* as critics have stated, nor as strictly *altruistic* as the professions themselves have claimed. For anyone interested in professional ethics, therefore, sensitivity to the shades and shadows of the moral life is important and can be developed through the study of basic skills of ethical analysis that we shall undertake in Chapter 3.

References and Suggestions for Further Reading

Bledstein, Burton J. 1976. *The Culture of Professionalism: The Middle Class and the Development of Higher Education in America.* New York: W. W. Norton & Company, Inc. A critique of professional pretensions.

Casselman, O. H. 1949. *Labor Dictionary.* New York: Philosophical Library. See the standard definition of *profession* on p. 376.

Cushman, Robert. 1975. "Let's Put Our House in Order: A Businessman's Plea," *Business and Society Review* XVL, pp. 49-52.

Dodson, Dan W. 1959. "Occupational Therapy for What? A Look at Values," *American Journal of Occupational Therapy* XIII (4): 189.

Durkheim, Emile. 1958. *Professional Ethics and Civil Morals,* trans. by Cornelia Brookfield. Glencoe, Ill.: Free Press.

Elliott, Philip. 1972. *The Sociology of the Professions.* London: MacMillan Press.

Greenwood, Ernest. 1957. "Attributes of a Profession," *Social Work* II (3), pp. 45-55. The cultural aspects of a profession.

Herrick, Robert L. 1978. "Comments and Discussion: Further Remarks on Professionalism." *Business and Professional Ethics* I (4) : p. 2.

Illich, Ivan. 1976. *Medical Nemesis: The Expropriation of Health.* New York: Pantheon Books. Modern medicine portrayed as a threat to health. Controversial.

————. 1977. *Toward a History of Needs.* New York: Pantheon Books. Disputation against professions as cartels.

Kotelchuck, David, ed. 1976. *Prognosis Negative: Crisis in the Health Care System.* New York: Random House, Inc.

Magee, John B. 1971. *Philosophical Analysis in Education.* New York: Harper and Row, Publishers. *Profession* defined, pp. 93-94.

Moore, Wilbert E. 1970. *Professions: Roles and Rules.* New York: Russell Sage Foundation.

Parsons, Talcott. 1968. "Professions." *International Encyclopedia of the Social Sciences.* Vol. XII, pp. 536-47. New York: Macmillan Co. and Free Press. An excellent instance of a technical sociological understanding of the profession, with substantial concern for ethics.

Pernick, Martin S. 1978. "Medical Professionalism," *Encyclopedia of Bioethics,* Warren T. Reich, ed. New York: Free Press, pp. 1028-1034. Contains an instructive functional definition of *profession.*

Soble, Alan. 1978. "Comments and Discussions: Some Remarks on Professionalism," *Business and Professional Ethics* I (3) : pp. 9-10.

West, Wilma L. 1968. "Professional Responsibility in Times of Change," *The American Journal of Occupational Therapy* XXII (1) : pp. 9-15.

Think More About It

1. Is the character of a professional organization (a) the sum of the characters of its members or is it (b) a moral entity in its own right? Explain why you choose (a) or (b).

2. Name some work groups included within *profession* in our restricted sense of the term. Name some that are excluded. Is the restricted

concept of *profession* helpful in thinking about certain kinds of work groups and in distinguishing them from others? Why or why not?

3. In your judgment, are professions as groups more exploitative of clients and society now than in earlier times in this or in the last century? If yes, what are some reasons for this trend? How can it be counteracted?

THREE

The Art of Ethics

Already we have been doing ethics. We have listened carefully to the voices of professions and professionals and discovered two moral themes characteristic of their work: *enablement* and *exploitation*. But the discovery of such themes, though important, is not the end of professional ethics. One needs to learn about major types of ethics and how they can apply to problems in professional life. In this brief space we cannot dip deeply into ethical theory, but we shall learn enough to enable professionals to deal *reflectively* with the moral dimensions of their work, and *effectively* as well.

EXPRESSIVE ETHICS — THE ETHICS OF CHARACTER

A patient once said admiringly of his physician, "He's a *real* professional." What he meant was not just that his doctor was superb technically, but that he conformed well to the character pattern regarded as fitting for a medical practitioner. Character is basic to all ethics and to professional ethics in particular, and it is regarded as such by the clientele.

Because we are able to think about ourselves and our own values more easily than about abstract theories of ethics, it is reasonable to begin our exploration of ethics with this topic.

Character ethics can well be regarded as *expressive ethics*. The question could be put, "What moral values do you wish to manifest through your life and practice?" This perspective emphasizes what one chooses or decides to be, as well as what a person *is*, in essence, prior to the moment of decision.

Character also refers to links between the person's past and future. For instance, if the accountant or therapist or teacher had strong character, one could count on him or her being at least fundamentally the same person in the next year as in the last, particularly with respect to some dominant traits or virtues. Such a person would make consistent moral decisions in similar situations at different times.

The problem of good professional character can be put like this. If you assume with St. Paul, St. Augustine, Thomas Hobbes, John Calvin, and a number of other moral thinkers, that human beings are fundamentally and naturally selfish, what is to keep professionals from devouring their clients rather than helping them? Not all the ethics codes in the world, for they will be ignored. Not even laws, since the courts and police enforcing them will be as corrupt as the law-breaking professionals. Instead, naked self-interest must be balanced with loving service, or the vices must be changed to virtues—transformed, if you will. Bad character must be refashioned into good so that professionals, at least the great bulk of them, will be inwardly and spontaneously motivated to positive ethical practice.

These issues can be illustrated by two contrasting examples of professional behavior. A physician in general practice was accused of running a "Medicaid Mill." He was reported to have processed a very high volume of elderly patients in his office, billing for professional treatment when the patients were in fact seen only by nonprofessional helpers. The prosecutor charged that he was billing for his own services even for occasions when he was out of town. His mother was charged with complicity in the racket; she was alleged to have been in charge of the billing operation. This is an apparent case of full-scale vice.

Contrast this calculated pattern of exploitation to the expression of *enablement* in the lives of a certain professional couple. The husband, a Ph.D. in agronomy, held a good-paying and secure position as a university agricultural extension agent in a delightful American valley. His wife, an M.D., had developed a private practice there. But they became aware of the challenge of world hunger, decided to leave their comfortable lives in America, and took positions in Africa to help in rural agricultural development in a poverty-stricken land. Character ethics seeks to help persons to avoid the moral errors in the first example and to embrace the good of the second.

Character ethics seeks to promote the good by commending to all persons the cultivation of *virtues* or *moral excellences*. Of the many possible moral virtues, tradition has distilled four cardinal or natural virtues from ancient Greek civilization: *justice, prudence, temperance,* and *courage. Justice* means a fair distribution of costs and benefits, *prudence* a due regard for one's own welfare and wisdom in handling one's affairs, *temperance* a moderate way of life and self-control, and *courage* the ability to face danger for the sake of principle. To the cardinal virtues theologians added the "theological" virtues of *faith, hope,* and *love—faith* meaning the confidence that the unseen truths of God are real, *hope* that the future will be superior in a significant way to the past, and *love* that one ought to give of oneself and one's skills to others in need.

Keeping these standards in mind, one can make some important judgments about professional behavior. For instance, referring to the case of the "Medicaid Mill," it seems quite clear that the physician and his mother lacked commitment to a number of the virtues. They were not committed to justice or they could not have billed the Medicaid program for services which they had not supplied. Certainly their actions did not embody love, because they were using others for their own ends rather than serving the needs of their patients. If one were to think that the mother–son team was prudent because they were looking out for their own interests, this, too, would be mistaken, because they failed to take into full account the risks of legal penalties and professional sanctions. On the other hand, the practices of many professionals, including the economic-development workers described above, express one or more of the virtues.

Not only do the virtues individually help us in thinking about professional ethics, but so do the virtues taken together in relationship to each other. Perhaps only saints embody all of the virtues, and even though most professionals aim at a more modest level of moral achievement, a balanced ensemble of virtues is a realistic goal. The basic point can be put in terms of developmental psychology: a professional must be a *whole person*.

I learned something about this from two former students. When we talked, one was about halfway through a course of graduate professional studies in a school of theology. He described the pressures built into that system of education toward encouraging students to devote all of their energies to becoming professionally competent, certified, and credentialed, to the exclusion, he felt, of the possibility of achieving completeness or wholeness as persons. Another student, this one in chemistry, reported how a graduate professor had dominated his life and those of the student's colleagues. Not only did the professor demand long hours of laboratory work, about 60 hours per week, but he even wanted to know how students were spending their nonlaboratory hours to make sure they remained focused upon study and research. This young man felt his personal wholeness slipping away to the point where he had to confront his professor with the demand to let him run his own life. He began to spend time once again with his spouse in bicycling and church work. Wholeness returned.

For the achievement of good character, wholeness is important. Professionals who sense the need to ground themselves in personal wholeness learn to channel energies away from sheer professional achievement to broader personal possibilities. They take up sports. They may devote themselves to children through the Y.M.C.A. or Scouting. They read widely. They cultivate the enjoyment of some sort of beauty through gardening or painting or listening to music. They develop a spiritual unity at the core of their personality.

It is the pursuit of a comprehensive basic life-theme that can make a person complete and also unite the professional virtues into a harmonious medley. Thomas Kelly (1957, p. 105) states this theme in the language of religious devotion:

> The outer distractions of our interests reflect an inner lack of integration of our own lives. We are trying to be several selves at once, without all our selves being organized by a single, mastering life within us. Each of us tends to be, not a single self, but a whole committee of selves.

What is the basic theme that would ideally characterize professionals? The old classical virtue of *love, beneficence,* or *other-regard,* is probably the theme that could best unify a squabbling committee of selves. Some three centuries ago an English writer, William Law (Quoted at Paton, 1968, p. 65), provided an enduring description of this moral trait:

> By love I do not mean any natural tenderness, which is more or less in people according to their constitution; but I mean a larger principle of the soul, founded in reason and piety, which makes us tender, kind, and gentle to all our fellow-creatures as creatures of God and for his sake.

Love is the enlargement of one's personal boundaries to facilitate the achievement of personal wholeness by other human beings. It is the backbone of moral style and character for professional life.

Many would question whether the virtues, capped by love, "work" in a professional setting. A manager with a large corporation says that his home life and friendships are one thing: other-regard would appropriately apply there. But at work defensiveness, politics, and intrigue fill the day. Love and the virtues are difficult to follow as a life-theme in the corporate jungle. The same seems true in professional political life as illustrated convincingly in Alan Alda's film *The Seduction of Joe Tynan.* The chief character, Senator Tynan, was constantly torn between his concern for his wife and children and the need to survive and flourish amidst powerful political pressures. His commitment to political life appeared to result from a genuine concern for his constituents and their welfare. Like a log in a wild winter surf he was tossed this way and that as he fought to balance competing claims on his life. One felt throughout the film that wholeness was his goal, and at the end that perhaps he had grasped it. But it was a fight all the way.

Perhaps professionals other than managers and politicians might find other-regard more readily applicable in their setting: teachers in relationship to students, medical practitioners to patients, and even lawyers to clients, for example. Business management may be the test case. At this point, however, we may assume that love, beneficence, or other-regard, understood as including conflict and enlightened self-interest, is an appropriate basic life-theme for professionals, even those in business.

Business persons, to paraphrase Alfred North Whitehead, should not think lightly of their tasks.

Character ethics brings certain insights that help us to better understand the theme of *enablement,* identified earlier as a moral theme common to the professions. First, character ethics resonates positively with the idea of enablement by conveying a certain sense of calmness in doing the right thing and courage in resisting the wrong. Second, character ethics gives one a measure of discretion in planning a course of moral action; it leaves the final judgment up to the individual. However, precisely in the individuality of character ethics lies one of its weaknesses for understanding the theme of enablement. As we learned previously, one must probe social and institutional moral values and not just the inner lives of individuals to understand adequately the professional life. Also, character ethics as we have interpreted it requires further explanation of the principles that help define justice. Consequently we must regard the ethics of character as one way, but not the only way, of thinking about the moral dimensions of the professional life and turn our attention to the ethics of our obligation to guide action by principle.

ETHICS OF OBLIGATION

If one of the weaknesses of character ethics is the failure to specify with clarity what one ought to do, that deficiency is satisfied to some extent by another type, the ethics of obligation. This type of ethics seeks to articulate the principles of moral laws that govern human life. One might think of it as the philosophical equivalent of jurisprudence, the science of law, insofar as it lays down rules that pertain to all persons. Various terms have been used to refer to this type of ethics: *duty* is one, *deontology* is another. As *deontos* in Greek means "obligation," we have chosen the label of the *ethics of obligation.*

Many examples of the ethics of obligation are found in the religious and philosophical heritage of humankind. Among them is the notion of *dharma (law* or *duty)* in Buddhist and Hindu thought as well as the *Shari'a* (Quranic law) in Islam. A clear example with which Western persons may be more familiar is the Ten Commandments, found in the Hebrew Scriptures and shared by Christians and Muslims. In 14 short verses in Exodus

20, four rules concerning one's relationship with God and six
more governing interaction with family and neighbors are deft-
ly set forth. The Scriptures trace a direct link between one's
relationship to God and consequent obligations to human
beings.

A second example of the ethics of obligation comes from the
medieval period of Europe, with roots reaching far back into
Roman and Greek times. Many Roman and Greek philosophers
felt that the primary moral understandings about life were to be
reached through using human reason to investigate truth. Their
naturalism is thus very different in spirit than the *revelationism*
of the Hebrew people. But Europeans during the Middle Ages
traced their heritage back to both of these two great sources—
Graeco-Roman philosophy and the Christian Scriptures. And
they resolved the difference in spirit between *naturalism* and
revelationism by agreeing that human reason carried the search
up to a certain level, but that God revealed additional truth beyond that level. *Natural law* was for medieval Europeans the universal moral principles that could be discerned through unaided
human reason; higher principles called *divine law* also existed
and were known by humans only through revelation.

The development of the system of natural law came to its full-
est fruition in the moral philosophy of Thomas Aquinas, the
towering thirteenth-century theologian. Centering ultimately in
God but embracing all of creation, this vast system defined moral
obligations for every facet of human life, including not only the
church but family and commercial life as well. The object was to
articulate principles that guided life in general, and the life of
each person in particular, to the highest degree of fulfillment.
Its influence lives on particularly in the moral theology of the
Roman Catholic Church, though in very recent decades great
diversity has emerged in the ethical thought of this church.

A third significant attempt to express moral insight in an
ethic of obligation was undertaken in Germany, after the redis-
covery of the power of reason in the Renaissance and subsequent
to the growth of science, by the eighteenth-century German
philosopher Immanuel Kant. Like the Greeks and Romans, Kant
began with the tools of reason only, not relying on revelation
at all. Kant summarized his discovery in terms of the *categorical
imperative*, the one rule that every rational being must obey.

"So act that the maxim of your action may be willed as a universal law," is the command of reason obeyed by every person of good will, said Kant. This one principle and its derivatives were, he held, sufficient to guide all of one's moral life.

The steps necessary in using Kant's imperative can be simplified as follows. First, clarify the proposed action: exactly what action is being considered? Next, state the maxim of the action, or the underlying rule of the behavior. Third, universalize the maxim, considering it as a law to be obeyed by all people at all times. Fourth, ask whether the law thus proposed is logically consistent or self-contradictory.

Some of the strengths and weaknesses of the ethics of obligation can be understood by reflecting on the following.

> An independent business person in the machinery fabricating business learns that his chief competitor is selling equipment to customers that they do not really need and that will not do the stipulated task. Should he tell his customers the truth about the fraud being perpetrated on them by this unscrupulous salesperson?

Each of our examples of the ethics of obligation would deliver an answer, though through different lines of reasoning. The Ten Commandments state, "You shall not bear false witness against your neighbor." By keeping silent our business person with the quandary would not be telling an expressed lie; apparently this would be in keeping with the commandment. Silence would be an attractive route for him because he has learned that exposing the misdeeds of a competitor is often resented, strangely enough, as a kind of unfair tactic even by the customer one is trying to help. On the other hand, perhaps the commandment ought to be read to the effect that one ought always to tell the full truth.

Kant has a way of resolving the ambiguity in such a situation. For Kant, one should not merely refrain from falsehood but should test the morality of the act by using the four-step procedure stated above. In this case the maxim of the proposed action is that one should inform one's customers about the full implications of a bill of goods being sold to them under false pretenses by a competitor. Can one universalize this maxim logically? Apparently so, since there is no contradiction involved in willing that prospective buyers learn the full truth in such situations through the competitive sales process. As a double-check, the maxim that a salesperson should never disclose the full truth about false claims made by a competitor, the universalized form of the rule underlying the alternative act, cannot be held logically because it contradicts much of the very nature of commercial interaction, which must proceed on the basis of honest disclosure about merchandise. Therefore, using the categorical imperative, our salesperson would apparently have to choose the route of informing the customer, even at the risk of being regarded as a "rat."

The ethics of obligation undoubtedly has a great strength in the consistency it brings to ethical reflection and human action. The same principle or moral law applies to all similar situations, thus alleviating some of the uncertainties that might result from simply requiring that all individuals derive their own conclusions intuitively.

On the other hand, much of the apparent clarity seems to blur when one asks exactly how a particular principle applies in a certain case, as with the question about the meaning of lying to one's customer. Or, if the clarity is preserved, as through the use of the categorical imperative, then the ethics of obligation has the deficiency of staking all of morality on duty for duty's sake while ignoring the consequences of the act, whether beneficial or harmful. Perhaps telling the truth about a false bill of goods to a customer who is likely to be resentful and buy the merchandise anyway is actually less ethical than letting the competitor lie. When the customer is disappointed with the merchandise, his anger will be directed against the competitor, and wrongdoing will reap its own reward. Problems in applying rules to specific cases and failure to give due regard to the consequences of action are the reasons why many thinkers have looked for still other ways of reflecting about the moral life.

In terms of our theme of enablement, the ethics of obligation lays great stress on the imperative of doing the right thing, or at least on refraining from doing the wrong thing, for duty's sake. And among these duties is that of respecting other human beings for their own inherent worth. Forcefully, underscoring this point, Kant taught that another formulation of the categorical imperative is, "Always treat persons as ends in themselves, never as means only." This indicates that my customers or clients, for instance, can never be regarded only as my means of dumping merchandise and increasing my profit, but must always be respected for their own inherent value. This lasting impact of the ethics of obligation helps to preserve and safeguard the human dignity of professional relationships.

ETHICS OF ASPIRATION

A third type of ethics, which may address some of the difficulties of the ethics of character and of obligation, emphasizes making moral decisions in terms of the ends sought. Sometimes this type of ethics is called *teleological,* a term derived from the word *telos,* Greek for *end* or *goal.* In using this type of ethic one *aspires* to act in such a way as to bring about a qualitatively better state of affairs.

Here the key question is, obviously, what desirable state of affairs should we aspire to? One has to have some criterion by which to distinguish between possible futures in terms of their moral qualities. We shall survey two answers that have been commonly given—the greatest good for the greatest number, and the kingdom of God.

In the nineteenth century the great English social philosopher and reformer, John Stuart Mill, articulated an ethics of aspiration called *utilitarianism,* a moral philosophy of great importance for social and professional policy in the past two centuries. Briefly, Mill taught that persons and organizations ought to gauge their actions in such a way as to bring about the greatest good for the greatest number, it being understood that "good" suggested not merely "happiness," but those forms of happiness of the highest quality. Thus our salesperson in a quandary would have to determine the relevant persons and publics that might be influenced by his action in the long term or short term. These would include at least himself, his own firm, his dependents, the competitor's firm, the entire industry, the consumers immediately in question, perhaps the relevant regulatory agencies, and even the general public. He would have to ask what sorts of benefits and harms would result for each person and group and seek the action that would produce the greatest good overall.

Utilitarianism clarifies something important about the meaning of *enablement* as a theme for the professions. Enablement, as

understood from this perspective, is a term that relates not only
to clients and customers, but also to one's own family, one's
agency, one's nation, and perhaps even humanity in general.
Utilitarianism has the great merit of forcing one to pay attention to all of the relevant circles of influence. The professional is
an *enabler* ultimately of all humankind, even though one's attention might be directed very close to home during most of the
working day.

One can quickly detect one weakness of utilitarianism, however, as soon as one seeks to work through a particular case. Our
salesperson does not know, in advance, exactly how a customer
might react to a specific action. For instance, if the salesperson
"blows the whistle" on the competitor, the customer might react
with feelings of deep appreciation, but it is also possible that
the honesty might be misunderstood as an unfair sales tactic and
resented. The uncertainties of human nature and history make
the calculation of future consequences difficult.

Religious forms of the ethics of aspiration occur in addition
to the more strictly philosophical versions. Within this century
the Social Gospel movement and liberation theology have sprung
up as ways of conceiving of better states of human affairs in
religious terms. Liberation theology, a recent movement identified
primarily with Roman Catholics in Latin America, aims to free
people from their oppressors in order to allow them to develop
into the complete persons that God wishes them to become. Various oppressors have been identified, according to the circumstances, but dictatorial governments, neocolonialism, capitalism,
and multinational corporations have been the "villains" most
often named.

Liberation theology has marked resemblance to an earlier religious ethic, based in American Protestantism, called the Social
Gospel. The objective of the Social Gospel movement was to re-
structure society in such a way that the kingdom of God, or
social salvation, would be realized to a more complete degree.
This powerful movement, reaching a peak about the turn of the
twentieth century, gave impetus to social reform and unionism
and tended to provide moral backing for the Democratic Party.
In many respects the great civil rights crusade of the 1960s,
led by Martin Luther King Jr. and others, was in direct line of
descent from the Social Gospel movement.

Among the many difficulties with these religious forms of the ethics of aspiration, just as with utilitarianism, is that an action calculated to bring about a better state of affairs might unexpectedly and unintentionally result in an overall worse effect. Another difficulty from the perspective of ethics for the the professions is that many professionals will not feel compelled by the religious worldview in which the ethics of liberation or of the Social Gospel are set.

One of the effects of this ethical perspective, however, is that it introduces an element of suspicion into the reflection of professionals that perhaps they are the *enemy*, not the friend, of their clients and the human family. The Social Gospel and liberation theology suggest very strongly that morality is tied to social class. The dominant ethics of any age and nation is normally a legitimating screen to mask the oppressive action of the dominant class, and professionals in management, medicine, teaching, and all other categories are or may be the unwitting agents of exploitation even while expounding an ethic of enablement. In this perspective enablement means to turn one's back on the upper and middle classes and devote one's professional skills to freeing the oppressed. In short, their middle- and upper-class status alone should give professionals cause to question themselves, according to these liberation ethics.

Before leaving the ethics of aspiration, we need to give very brief attention to *egoism,* the ethics of self-interest. In this individualistic version of consequentialism the primary question to be asked of the alternative proposed actions is, "Which action will bring the greatest long-term benefit to me?" The good is identified with one's own personal fortunes. An outsider looking at such an "ethic" will say that it is no ethic at all, since it recognizes no mutual obligations among parties. It is immoral, such an observer would judge, because it is merely a strategy for aggrandizement and overlooks such factors as the common good, the kingdom of God, or the principles to be obeyed. In this "ethic" the classical vices come to be regarded as virtues.

Yet this egoistic philosophy is very attractive today, indicated by the plethora of books on assertiveness, intimidation, and "looking out for Number One." It is highly possible that large numbers are in the professions or entering them precisely because clients generally have a childlike reverence for superior authority and can very easily be intimidated and controlled. In less extreme language, individuals might be attracted to the professions primarily for reasons of social status or high and stable incomes. These, too, could be indicative of egoistic aspirations.

In due course we shall give more thorough consideration to egoism. At this point, however, we shall return to our main theme and face the issue which is probably most pressing in the mind of every reader—namely, how am I to choose an ethic for myself, given that each has its inherent weaknesses as well as strengths?

ETHICS OF RESPONSIBILITY

Given the uncertainties inherent in each of these ethical systems, how can I choose the one that is right for me and my professional practice? This must be answered in terms of the nature of the systems themselves and of decision making in practice.

As to the systems themselves, many concerned with ethical decision making in daily practice have found that the formal versions of moral reflection are more relevant to the ivory tower than to the hustle and bustle of practical life. They have concluded, in other words, that the great systems were designed by scholars mainly for their own consumption, with a built-in gap between scholarly standards and the world of work. It is difficult to apply the systems to daily practice because they conform to the thought-world of the academy.

It is true that professional academics, by and large, have been responsible for the formulation of the great ethical systems. It would seem highly dangerous to assume that this in itself means that the systems are inapplicable to daily life, however, since applied science is also a scholarly product. In fact, some of the systems introduced above originated not in the ivory tower but in the laboratory of social struggle, to be refined only later in an academic setting. But probably the clarity of the great systems has been achieved, like an experiment in a controlled environment, by eliminating some variables that would cloud the issues in real life. If so, then it would follow that decisions in daily practice will never be accompanied by the degree of clarity conveyed in the great systems, but also that the systems can help to bring greater clarity to daily life. The systems are tools for clarifying moral reflection.

It may help to recognize that many astute people in actual practice use a mix of types of ethics. In day-to-day situations they may operate with reference to a set of principles that are perhaps even only somewhat dimly perceived. When they face unique, nonrepetitive decisions, they may bring calculations of consequences into operation. If really pushed to the wall in a situation in which they cannot compromise, they may act according to principle without any regard to consequences. As people mature in decision making they achieve an artful ability to make appropriate ethical responses by drawing selectively from their repertoire of ethical knowledge.

Ethics in practice seems at best to be an *art of informed judgment activated by a benevolent spirit.* When we are confronted by morally alert persons who lead practical lives, we notice that they know something of the vocabulary and major systems of formal ethics. The art of ethics for them involves a process of wisely selecting tools for reflection from their store of vocabulary, concepts, and frameworks. Personal style, taste, and emotional response all enter into this art, along with the willingness to decide and act even though these morally alert persons may never achieve complete certainty about their best course of action.

We may conclude that in practical life there is no single type of ethics that is guaranteed to produce better judgments than all others. Practitioners of the benevolent spirit and informed judgment may have to settle for less theoretical clarity than the mind yearns for. There is no assurance that a perfectly good decision can be attained. Decisions must be made even at some degree of risk by selecting the ideas that best clarify the situation, aiming at responsible action. To alter one of Martin Luther's epigrams: people must reflect, then act bravely.

To convey some idea of the art of doing applied ethics, the following scheme will help. It is provided here as an example; the pattern could well vary from person to person, situation to situation.

I am presented with the information that some members of the American public cannot purchase the services of my profession despite their genuine need.

1. Is this an ethical issue?

At first it appears to be an economic issue, but when I apply the test of justice, I conclude that perhaps services are not being distributed with due regard to real need. Therefore this economic issue has an ethical dimension.

2. What is going on?

My information comes from an article in a national news weekly. I carefully reread the article, noting that the immediate problem has been caused by a change in federal welfare subsidies to states. I try to find further information about the situation from competent authorities such as social scientists and experienced administrators.

3. How does the situation bear on general meanings of life?

I try to determine what the changes mean to the various parties —the recipients, the legislators, the general public, and myself. I remain open to unfamiliar meanings that I might encounter in my investigation.

4. What help can I get from my knowledge of ethics?

I review the ethics of obligation, aspiration, and character. I write down concepts and frameworks that I have selected as being especially important in attaining greater clarity about the underlying moral dimensions of the situation.

5. Can other persons help me to broaden my moral horizon?

I discuss the situation with trusted friends and colleagues, in or out of my profession, and especially with some in the affected group of poor people.

6. What shall I decide?

After this process of reflection, I decide on my course of action, aiming to achieve the most fitting response. I may decide to change my own personal practice in some way, and I may further determine to influence my profession, firm, government, or attitudes in society.

7. How shall I act?

Action is integral to doing ethics. I act in accordance with my decision in Step 6. The action might involve a short-term or a long-term plan or strategy.

8. In review, do I approve of my understanding and action?

Review is as important as initial reflection. Through reviewing I learn of changes needed in my understanding or actions, and of the success and/or failure of my process of doing ethics.

The scenario above is general and can be adapted or refined. Since ethics is an art, the process has to be shaped and adapted by each person or group in each situation. When professionals have to make decisions quickly, entire components in the procedure may have to be deferred until after the decision is made to be brought up later. Particularly in the case of a serious and troubling issue, the process of reflecting, deciding, acting, and reviewing may continue in repeated cycles for years.

CONCLUSION

We are now in a position to refine our understandings of professions and professionals, and of enablement as the theme of the professions. From our present perspective we could say that ideally a *profession* should be *an association of skilled workers with broad, general knowledge, bound together by ethical policies oriented toward enablement.* A *professional* is *a highly skilled worker with a broad outlook, belonging to an association of colleagues, upholding its standards of practice and sharing its commitment to enablement. Enablement,* the moral theme of the professions as amplified by considerations in this chapter, means *compassionate and informed service of the needs of clients and of successively broader circles of society, guided by careful reflection on the moral meaning of one's action so as to achieve increasingly fitting forms of practice.*

Neither most professions nor professionals conform to these ideal definitions in their entirety. In many cases the gap is flagrant. However, the purpose of normative definitions such as these is not to describe things as they are but to project things as they might and ought to be. These definitions are rooted in tradition, and if professions do not measure up today, the reason may well be that they have lost sight of their own true significance.

An ethic of responsibility in which principles and consequences are considered while aiming for an appropriate action seems the most sensible and defensible approach to professional ethics. Enlightened professionals will select appropriate goals, seek good consequences, and formulate good sets of principles on the basis of good character. They will be able to think creatively about each unique situation without losing sight of an overarching frame of reference. This sensitive style of ethics does not come automatically to anyone, least of all to those who have wrapped themselves in the protective mantle of professionalism. Instead it results from self-discipline and a carefully nurtured vision of the nature of things. In the end professional ethics is a wholistic art of exercising informed good judgment.

References and Suggestions for Further Reading

Albert, Ethel M., Theodore C. Denise, Sheldon P. Peterfreund. 1957. *Great Traditions in Ethics: An Introduction.* New York: American Book Company. One of many collections to which beginning students can turn for excerpts from, and commentary and bibliography for, classical ethical systems.

Bertocci, Peter A. and Richard M. Millard. 1963. *Personality and the Good: Psychological and Ethical Perspectives.* New York: David McKay Company, Inc. A philosophical treatment of the concept of character.

Bok, Sissela. 1979. *Lying: Moral Choice in Public and Private Life.* New York: Vintage Books. A recent statement of applied, as distinct from formalistic, ethics.

Campbell, Alastair V. 1975. *Moral Dilemmas in Medicine: A Coursebook in Ethics for Doctors and Nurses.* Edinburgh: Churchill Livingstone, second ed.

Frankena, William K. 1973. *Ethics.* Englewood Cliffs, N.J.: Prentice-Hall, Inc., second ed. A standard survey of philosophical ethics.

Hauerwas, Stanley. 1975. *Character and the Christian Life: A Study in Theological Ethics.* San Antonio: Trinity University Press. A religious treatment of the concept of character.

Kelly, Thomas. 1957. *A Testament of Devotion.* London: Hodder and Stoughton.

La Croix, W. L., S.J. 1979. *Principles for Ethics in Business.* Washington, D.C.: University Press of America, rev. ed.

Niebuhr, Richard. 1963. *The Responsible Self: An Essay in Christian Moral Philosophy*. New York, Evanston, and London: Harper & Row. A primary source for the ethics of responsibility.

Ogletree, Thomas W. 1980. "The Activity of Interpreting in Moral Judgment," *Journal of Religious Ethics* VIII:1. A recent statement of the ethics of responsibility. Technical vocabulary; complete bibliography.

Paton, Alan. 1968. *Instrument of Thy Peace*. New York: Seabury Press.

Swomley, John M., Jr. 1972. *Liberation Ethics*. New York: Macmillan Company. For further reading on liberation theology and ethics.

Rauschenbusch, Walter. 1917. *A Theology for the Social Gospel*. New York: Abingdon Press.

Think More About It

1. Interview a professional about the role of character in his or her work. What new perspectives on the meaning and importance of character do you obtain from this conversation?

2. Scan a week's editions of a major newspaper with the concept of professional character in mind. Clip articles that document abuses and condemnations and/or positive examples and commendations. What patterns seem to dominate the news?

3. Write a brief essay on professional character, using an actual person known to you as the example. This person may be either of especially good or bad character. Briefly define professional character as you understand it. Then describe the character of the particular professional you have in mind, using specific instances where appropriate. Finally, briefly state a judgment on how the person you wrote about matches or does not match the model of professional character you set up in the first paragraph or two.

FOUR

Professional Ethics Codes and Committees

In our summary of the framework of professional ethics so far we have noted that *enablement* is a moral theme indigenous to the professions but that one needs a degree of knowledge of traditional ethics in order to apply this theme with skill and confidence to the problems that professionals face. We have identified the very real possibility before all professions and professionals of falling into exploitative patterns. As Henri Nouwen has said, "All those who want to reach out to their fellow human beings in the context of one of the many helping professions . . . have to keep reminding themselves that they do not own anyone who is in need of care" (Nouwen, 1975, p. 64).

It would seem that professional ethics codes could possibly provide for all of the needs mentioned. Virtually every profession has a code of professional ethics that sets out expectations for behavior, and such codes are sufficiently important for our topic that we include them here as the fourth major element in the framework of professional ethics. But before assuming that codes are sufficient to guarantee satisfactory moral performance, we need to familiarize ourselves with them and then ask some questions. We would need to know with what moral authority they are written, something about their main concerns, and whether they are implemented in such a way as to be reflected significantly in daily practice. Let us, then, survey some representative ethics codes and the committees responsible for them.

In their work most professionals will be subject to at least two distinct kinds of ethics or conduct codes. One is the organizational conduct code. Corporations and large agencies often develop statements of corporate conduct to keep interactions among their employees at a certain moral level. We are not dealing with organizational conduct codes at this time. What we are dealing with here are codes produced by professional organizations to set out standards expected of their members, whether self-employed or on the payrolls of large organizations.

To be still more specific, we are dealing here with what we shall call "Modern Professional Ethics Codes, Generation II." It is important to realize that contemporary codes have historic precedents, one as much as 5500 years old. The Code of Hammurabi (3500 B.C.) and the Hippocratic Oath (c. 350 B.C.) are models for legal-commercial and medical ethics codes respectively. Thus our contemporary codes are products of a long, slow sedimentary process and represent both a gradual accumulation of the experience of the ages and shaping by contemporary social values, economic pressures, and political developments.

The distinction between Modern Generation I and II requires a comment. Modern Generation I codes, products of the early twentieth century, dealt with the etiquette of relationships between professionals—"one shall not speak ill of a colleague," and so forth. But, as Mila Aroskar (1980, p. 658) points out, "In the 1980s, this does not even touch on the complex ethical dilemmas faced by both individual nurses . . . and by the nursing profession itself." What is true for nurses is true for other professions as well. Modern Generation II codes deal with dilemmas rising out of new knowledge, new technology, and new social attitudes. They are post-World War II and post-Watergate.

CODES BY COMMITTEE — HOW WRITTEN, WITH WHAT AUTHORITY?

"Codes by committee" is what we have in the professions today. By contrast, as late as the nineteenth century leaders would produce codes as sole authors. Such appears to have been the case with Florence Nightingale's nursing code and many other earlier classical codes. They were either written by one person or, if produced by multiple authors, were given the name of a single leader to bring status and authority to the document. Today virtually no professional code has a single author. If the author is, in fact, a specific individual, this will be obscured for public purposes by claiming committee authorship when the code is published. What the committee produces is adopted by the entire professional organization by vote.

A typical writing procedure is as follows. A committee of a professional organization decides that a new code or revision is needed and prepares a resolution to the effect, authorizing a code committee to go to work. The organizational membership approves the resolution, and a code committee is selected. The committee works with prior codes of the same organization, recent codes of similar organizations, and suggestions for revision garnered from such sources as members' concerns and relevant legal actions. A preliminary draft of the new code is circulated for comment. When comments are received, the final form is fixed and sent to the entire membership of the organization for study prior to ratification and adoption.

Judged by ethical criteria we have reviewed so far, the writing process has both strengths and weaknesses. Among the strengths is the participatory nature of the process itself, especially that all parties are given the opportunity to help create and then to adopt the standards to which they are to be held accountable. Besides embodying an important principle of organizational development, this procedure is in keeping with the categorical imperative of Kant, which counsels respect for persons and recognition of their moral autonomy. In addition, the participatory process of code writing is an instance of the practice of social ethics because it involves institutionalizing certain moral values in the fabric of the professional organization itself.

Among the weaknesses of the process, the foremost shows up precisely in that only the membership participates in the writing process. Who is to ensure that the legitimate interests of the clientele or consumers are represented in the writing and adoption of the code? Or, for that matter, that the broader interests of society are defended? The structure of the writing process almost insures that the interests of the association and its members will be given the greatest weight. Although it may be argued that association members are also members of society, there are bound to be divided loyalties when ethical decisions impinge upon one's freedom to practice and collect fees. Enablement would be better served if representatives of the clientele and society-at-large were included in the process of writing the professional code.

CONCERNS OF THE CODES

Why write and publish codes? One obvious reason is for the guidance of the membership on ethical matters, and this is the most commonly stated purpose. For instance, we read in the preamble to the "Principles of Occupational Therapy Ethics": "They are intended to be action-oriented, guiding and preventing rather than negative or merely disciplinary." We have already seen an example of how this purpose is fulfilled by the code. Recall Lois, the C.P.A. introduced in Chapter 1; a code provided her with specific guidelines for making an appropriate decision and acting in a dilemma. A somewhat more inspiring statement appears in the "Code of Ethics and Professional Practices for Industrial Designers": "Unlike legal statutes that specify minimum standards of performance, an essential purpose of a code of ethics is to set before us higher goals, goals for achieving our best as designers." These are typical of the stated purpose of most codes—to respond to the professional's need for a standard or an ideal of personal high performance and excellence.

A second purpose is to protect the profession in one of two ways. First, codes are for disciplining the members through maintenance of standards. One of the explicit purposes of the Council of Better Business Bureaus, Inc., for instance, is to support the self-regulation of business (Wilkens, 1975, p. 63). Ideally every profession is self-regulating, and the code is instrumental in striving for this state of affairs.

Incompetence is a problem that plagues all professions. The medical professions, for example, have long been concerned to guard against the presence of quacks in their ranks. Quack, derived from the archaic word *quacksalver*, denotes an incompetent or untrained person claiming professional skills. The presence of such individuals in the ranks of a profession, if unchallenged, would endanger the public through the perpetration of false claims. A profession known to condone incompettence would lose public confidence and run the risk of increased governmental regulation. The price of professional self-government is responsible self-policing, and codes provide the standards by which the practice of professionals is judged.

The second, and more sinister, side of the protecting function of codes is that they can be used to give the profession undue leverage over the consumer. In such cases government may step in to redress the wrongs. Very recently, for instance, in a decision of significance for all professions, the Federal Trade Commission (F.T.C.) ruled that the ban in the American Medical Association code against physician advertising was a restraint against free trade. The F.T.C. determined that the code could have been used unfairly to protect the profession against the public's due interests. In this instance the law appears to have provided a higher moral standard than had the professional code.

Support for individual members is a third purpose of codes. Consider once again our C.P.A., Lois, having to justify the use of a conservative accounting method to her client. She could honestly say, "To use any other method would put me in noncompliance with the ethics code of my association." Insofar as few clients or employers would want to be known for pressuring professionals to violate their codes, their existence provides a measure of effective protection.

Unspoken purposes are important also. Marginal professions may adopt codes to give an air of greater professionalism to their group. Their purpose may be to promote good public relations, as distinct from professional practice. Another unspoken function of codes is to bring professions into the modern age, to bureaucratize them. Bureaucracies operate in accordance with formal rules. The form of codes is that of impersonal, objective rule statements. In this respect the growing number of formal professional ethics codes simply marks the modernization of the professions.

In short, in evaluating professional codes, one should seek to determine the explicit and implicit purposes and audiences for which they are written. As we have seen, the code may actually function as a smoke screen for unethical activities. It is for this very human reason that a person who has been extensively involved in the writing of such codes warned, "It's always essential to ask who the audience is."

Further considerations with respect to the content of the codes might be addressed to the major aspects of the moral life itself. Here, to organize our very brief survey, we would do well to adopt a three-fold division introduced by C. S. Lewis (1960, p. 71), the late English scholar. He would have us ask: what do the codes have to say about the inner moral life of the practitioner, the relationships between individuals, and the purpose of human life as a whole?

With respect to the first aspect, the codes in general pay scant attention to the issue of the inner life of the practitioner. The code of the American Physical Therapy Association discusses the character of practitioners, emphasizing solely their altruistic motives and openness. This seems naive because self-interest is certainly an important factor, and not to be overlooked. Similarly, the American Bar Association refers to the need of the lawyer to have good character, without analyzing in any detail its nature. The American Occupational Therapy Association says nothing on this score.

In reference to this very important dimension of ethics, the constitution of the individual, why do the codes say so little? An analysis of the form taken by the codes reveals that they contain primarily *rules* to guide action. The codes tend toward a very legalistic tone. But as stated already in Chapter 3, the mere existence of rules or laws will do little to promote desirable behavior unless the individuals who are to be guided are disposed to obey the rules. The writers of ethics codes seem to assume that the practitioners will be persons of sufficiently good character to be disposed to obey the rules. Though one would hope that the writers' assumption is justified, professional ethics committees probably ought to give more attention to a dimension of the moral life they now largely neglect—the harmonization of the inner life of the practitioner.

Far more coverage is awarded in the codes to the second area of the moral life, relationships between persons. The American Physical Therapy, Occupational Therapy, and Bar Association, and Industrial Designers Society of America codes, in fact, devote almost all of their space to duties toward clients, colleagues, employers, and the profession itself. Insofar as the codes spell out in detail one's duties to others, they are capable of serving as effective instruments of a style of enablement. Their main purpose seems to consist in forestalling exploitative relationships.

With respect to one aspect of relationships between persons, most codes are strangely silent. This point, however, must be of significance to all professionals—namely, what each of them as individuals can rightly hope to gain from their practices. The American Physical Therapy Association emphasizes altruistic motives and says nothing about the legitimate desires or self-interest of the professional that might be met through physical therapy practice. The American Occupational Therapy Association says nothing on the score. The Industrial Designers Society of America comments on the need to support "one another's interests"; this comes closer to the matter but still does not address what a designer can legitimately expect to receive from a practice. Only the American Management Associations' statement (not a true code) alludes to proper self-interest, and then only indirectly by affirming the "dignity and validity of the profit motive." Another observer, after noting this failure of the codes to comment on the degree to which the professional can take his own interests into account in decision making, asks, "Is it really plausible that the individual's interests are not relevant or that it is a simple matter how they are to be weighed against other factors?" He then notes, "In fact, many, if not most, occasions on which 'unprofessional' conduct is charged are ones in which the violator is alleged to have improperly favored his own interests" (Lockhart, 1980, p. 1).

The most probable reason for the lack of references to the professional's self-interest is the desire to maintain the ideology of service. We certainly support that theme. However, to be properly interpreted it would have to include an acknowledgment of legitimate self-interest and its limitations.

When one goes on to ask about the third main area of ethics identified by C. S. Lewis, that of the general purpose of human life or what we referred to as 'worldview' in Chapter 1, the Modern Generation II codes receive very low scores. For instance, the Council of Better Business Bureaus' code seems to have no reference to worldview at all, according to Paul Wilkens (1975, pp. 62-63.) The American Bar Association refers to the need for a healthy legal system, but surely this is not what we mean by

the general purpose of life. The American Occupational Therapy
Association comes closer to speaking of worldview in obliging
the therapist to take a "global view" of health in relation to the
emerging needs of society. But the American Management Associations and the Industrial Designers Society of America go the
furthest. The statement of the A.M.A. refers to supporting social
values and community welfare. The Industrial Designers Society
of America code refers to the enrichment of human well-being as
the purpose of the profession; this is potentially a rich and compelling vision.

A way to assess the worldviews of modern professions is to
compare them to professions at other times and in other places.
The basic worldviews expressed by professional codes from the
fourth century B.C. to the nineteenth A.D. were explicitly religious.
Here are some relevant passages, the first from the Oath of Hippocrates: "I swear by Apollo Physician, by Asclepius, by Health,
by Panacea, and by all gods and goddesses, making them my wit-
nesses, that I will carry out according to my ability and judgment,
this oath and this indenture." Next, the pledge of Maimonides, a
thirteenth-century Jewish philosopher-physician: "Thy eternal
providence has appointed me to watch over the life and health of
my fellow beings. . . . Here am I ready for my vocation and now I
turn unto my calling." And finally, from Florence Nightingale,
founder of the nursing profession: "I solemnly pledge myself
before God and in the practice of this assembly to pass my life
in purity and to practice my profession faithfully" (Cited by
Purtilo, 1977, pp. 1002-1003).[1] Those quotations are from other
times and places.

Now consider a profession in another place but in our own
time, the legal profession in Ghana, the West African state. Its
practice has been to commence its annual convention with a religious service. In October 1977, for instance, the Rev. C. G.
Baëta, an internationally known Ghanaian scholar, delivered the
sermon before the lawyers assembled for their Legal Year Service, in which he spoke of God's creation of man and the significance of human government and law in the light of man's crea-
turehood.

---

1. Reprinted from *Physical Therapy* (Vol. 57, 1002-1003) with the
permission of the American Physical Therapy Association.

In each instance cited from other times and cultures, the foundation of professional obligation is perceived as based in divine purposes, inclining the practitioner toward the liberation of others from disease and need. This is exactly what ethicists, anthropologists, philosophers, and other students of culture would expect to find. It fits the pattern of mutually implied relationships between religion and ethics found in most cultures.

In comparison to the older and foreign codes, American ones seem to have tunnel vision. Our modern codes, Generation II, are imbalanced as moral systems; they restrict themselves to providing rules without supplying an adequate supporting worldview. Professions seem to be riding on the shrinking religious capital of modern society, inherited from earlier generations, without contributing to its maintenance. Like society at large, professions are becoming secularized, but this may be a greater danger than is generally recognized.

One must be cautious in calling for a renewal of worldviews to underlie professional ethics for several reasons. First, no single religion could provide the worldview for a particular profession in our era; adherents of many faiths as well as nonbelievers populate every organization. Second, even many believers would be embarrassed, and perhaps justifiably, by religious affirmations as pointed as those in the classical codes quoted. Third, a mechanical reiteration of quaint worldviews, were that to occur, would have no value. And fourth, no religious organization should be placed in a position of being able to dictate to professional organizations, which are autonomous in nature.

However, a desirable approach to reconstructing a viable supporting worldview for professional ethics codes, even in our pluralistic age, seems possible. The challenge is to devise worldview statements that accommodate the pluralism of individual beliefs in our society, yet establish ground for a common call to free people from enslavement to need and for support of a just social order. The Industrial Designers Society of America seems to have pointed to a viable path with its affirmation of the enrichment of human life as the purpose of the profession. In exploring the lines suggested here, the authors of ethics codes would be justified to follow the precedent set years ago by Thomas Jefferson and other writers of the American Declaration of Independence when they formulated the classic mediating reference to the "laws of nature and nature's God."

In summary, our brief analysis points out that professional codes show much strength as rules-ethics, especially with respect to relationships between the professional and others. However they are deficient in several other ways. With such deficiencies, the codes could not be expected to give sufficient guidance to the professional. Consequently one must bring to professional decision making not only the resources of the appropriate code(s) but also of one's own skill in moral reflection.

PLATITUDES VERSUS PERFORMANCE

"Professional codes are all window dressing," critics might charge. "They provide platitudes without causing any real change in performance."

The mere existence of professional codes is surely no guarantee of the effective performance of the values expressed. During the Nazi era professional codes were not lacking, yet professions have never fallen into greater depths of sinister behavior. Likewise the code of the American Bar Association did not prevent lawyers surrounding President Nixon from committing disreputable acts. But what we wish to know is whether the existence of codes or programs for implementing them have any practical effect on professionals in more typical circumstances.

First, when it produces a code, each profession takes measures to get copies printed and into the hands of each member. Current members may be mailed copies, or the codes may be printed in journals which members receive. Newly received members will receive copies of the code upon application and may even be tested over the provisions before acceptance into membership.

However, common sense and informal evidence would lead one to surmise that many professionals do not seek to maintain a working knowledge of their respective codes. One class of students interviewed professionals of various disciplines to determine whether they were aware of their codes and found that less than 10 percent were even able to find copies in their offices. This informal evidence supports the suspicion that possession of the professional code is a low priority for most practitioners. A generous interpretation is that professionals by and large practice ethically as a matter of course; therefore, frequent reference to the code is unnecessary except in case of alleged infractions.

A second factor is that many professional organizations have standing committees concerned with ethics. The names of such committees vary: the American Physical Therapy Association's is designated the Judicial Committee, and educational organizations may have their Professional Standards Committee or Professional Ethics Committee. The duties of the standing committees include the revision of the ethics codes, educational campaigns on professional ethics, and consultations. But how effective are such committees? A survey of 64 professional societies in the scientific and engineering fields discovered that only about 12 percent did not have standing committees. However, only about one-third had staff offices to back up the committees, and slightly less had special funding for ethics activities. In these fields, then, only about one-third of all societies had truly effective measures for promoting professional ethics (A.A.A.S., 1980, p. 5).

A third standard for measuring the implementation of professional ethics would be whether organizations have any sanctions available for disciplining the membership. Some indication of the situation in science and engineering associations is revealed in that of 105 organizations with identifiable sanctions available, only half of them had imposed sanctions at any time between 1970 and 1979 (A.A.A.S., 1980, p. 6). Even then, the hearing process may be so secretive that peer-group leniency may be permitted. In law, after concluding that, "Self-regulation has lapsed," Martin Garbus and Joe Seligman (1976, p. 48) report that, "In 1972, bar associations disciplined 357 lawyers, or roughly one-tenth of one percent of the nation's 380,000 practicing lawyers."

Nevertheless, it is worth noting that ethics committees may and sometimes do act as quasi courts of law. The procedure typically begins with a complaint brought before the committee. The committee convenes as a hearing board, evidence is brought by the complainant and the respondent, and judgment is rendered. If the charge is sustained, a penalty could be assessed, ranging from reprimand through censure to a temporary or permanent lifting of one's certification. For a diagram of the flow of disciplinary procedures in the American Physical Therapy Association, see Figure 3.

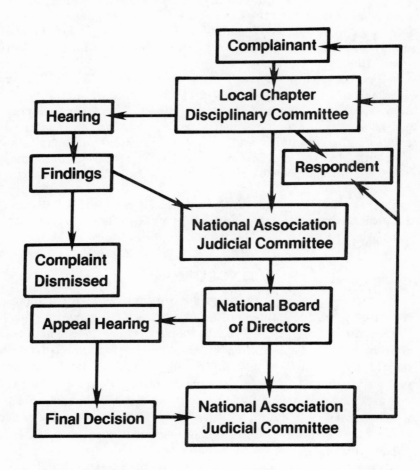

Figure 3. Simplified chart of the disciplinary action procedures of the American Physical Therapy Association.

In sum, then, does it seem likely that professional behavior is affected through the existence of ethics codes and implementation procedures? Our informal survey suggests that professional organizations need to work harder to bring the ethics codes into the daily life of professional practice so that professional ethics becomes part of their daily practice. Professional organizations could learn much from the experience of large business corporations, some of which, as we shall learn in Chapter 6, have achieved outstanding results in alerting employees to ethical-conduct expectations.

Before concluding that all the work involved in producing codes has simply gone for naught, one has to consider the possibility that the influence of codes is indirect. The sheer existence of a code within a professional organization, the fact that new members receive copies and read them at least once, and the possibility that the practitioners might refer to the codes in crisis situations all suggest the possibility of subtle but real indirect influence.

At this time, however, the candid observer must admit that the positive impact of the codes on professionals seems minimal and obscure.

CONCLUSION

The professions have far to go before they achieve reasonable effectiveness in the implementing of professional codes of ethics. Taking the matter of implementation first, much more should be done to publicize existing codes and the process that led up to their adoption. More time and funding should be devoted to investigating how to effectively educate memberships to the provisions and expectations of the codes. This may be an area in which professions stand to learn much from the performance of businesses and other large-scale organizations.

In addition, the professions ought to address their energies to certain typical deficiencies in codes. The first has to do with the cultivation of professional character. The rule-ethics typically found in codes will be of value only when persons of benevolent spirit inwardly wish to follow their guidance. The second relates to the need to clarify the degree to which professionals can take their self-interest into account in relationship to the needs of clients. The third is to ask what can be done to reground ethics in compelling worldviews instead of eliminating all references to the overarching purposes of life. The final point relates to a deficiency in the writing process: committees ought to devise means for client groups to contribute suggestions.

Even with codes tailored to make up for the deficiencies cited, their limitations will still be considerable. As A. V. Campbell (1975, p. 5) points out, the formulation of codes does not do away with or solve moral dilemmas in the professions. Rather, it may simply increase the awareness of professionals of the gravity of the dilemmas they face. Therefore professional ethics codes must always be complemented with skill in the art of ethics; these two are both necessary elements in the framework of professional ethics.

References and Suggestions for Further Reading

A.A.A.S. 1980. "A.A.A.S. Professional Ethics Project," *Business and Professional Ethics* III: 3 (Spring): pp. 5-6.

Aroskar, Mila A. 1980. "Anatomy of an Ethical Dilemma: The Theory." *American Journal of Nursing*, April, pp. 658-60. A carefully developed structure for consideration of ethical dilemmas in interdisciplinary settings.

Campbell, A. V. 1975. *Moral Dilemmas in Medicine.* Edinburgh: Churchill Livingstone, second ed.

Cushman, Robert. 1975. "Let's Put Our House in Order: A Businessman's Plea," *Business and Society Review* XVL, pp. 49-52. Contains a plea for an ethics committee for business.

Freedman, Monroe H. 1975. *Lawyers' Ethics in an Adversary System.* Indianapolis: Bobbs-Merrill Co. Examples of dilemmas and resolutions of them.

Garbus, Martin and Joe Seligman. 1976. "Sanctions and Disbarment: They Sit in Judgment," in *Verdicts on Lawyers,* ed. Ralph Nader and Mark Green. New York: Thomas Y. Crowell Co., pp. 47-60.

Kaserman, Imogene. 1977. "A Nursing Committee and the Code for Nurses." *American Journal of Nursing*, May, pp. 875-876. The development of the Tennessee Nurses' Association procedures for dealing with code violations.

Keane, Mark E., moderator. 1975. "A Post-Watergate Code of Ethics," *Public Management* LVII (6): pp. 7-12.

Kuhn, James W. 1977. "Socially Responsible Business: Its Past and

Future." *Church and Society* LXVII, No. 4 (March-April): pp. 5-11.

Lewis, C. S. 1960. *Mere Christianity*. New York: Macmillan Company, rev. ed.

Lockhart, T. W. 1980. "Professional Societies and the Enforcement of Professional Codes," *Business and Professional Ethics* III: 3 (Spring), pp. 1-3.

Nader, Ralph and Mark Green, eds. 1976. *Verdicts on Lawyers*. New York: Thomas Y. Crowell Co. Negatively biased but insightful and well-researched, with suggestions for improvements of ethics standards.

Nouwen, Henri J. M. 1975. *Reaching Out: The Three Movements of the Spiritual Life*. Garden City, N.Y.: Doubleday and Co., Inc.

Purtilo, Ruth B. 1977. "The American Physical Therapy Association's Code of Ethics." *Physical Therapy* 57 (9): pp. 1001-1006. A historical interpretation of the newly revised code.

Wilkens, Paul L. 1975. "The Case for Ethical Absolutes in Business." *Business and Society Review* XII: pp. 61-63. Describes attempts at industry-wide code development.

Think More About It

1. Interview a professional you know about his or her use of the professional ethics code. Does the person have a copy of the code at hand? Does he know the provisions of the code?

2. Why, among all the professions, has business management failed to develop a professional code with wide acceptance? What practical problems, if any, does this deficiency create for business relative to other professions?

PART TWO

THE
CONTEMPORARY SETTING
OF
PROFESSIONAL ETHICS

FIVE

Professions in a Technological Era

The *milieu* of the modern professions is dominated by technology and bureaucracy. These factors are of great importance for ethics; they shape the nature of moral problems. Part Two is devoted to the contemporary context of professional ethics. In Chapter 5 we shall deal with modern technology; in Chapter 6 we shall raise questions about modern bureaucracy.

The interdependence between modern technology and the professions has enormously enhanced the power and prestige of the professions, increasing their opportunities for greater enablement as well as for exploitation of clienteles and society. When technology increases one's "kit" of professional tools and techniques, it thereby multiplies one's power and responsibility.

TECHNOLOGY—KNOWLEDGE AND CONTROL

Consider briefly the old picture of technology and its distinction from science. Who was the scientist? A recluse, a gowned searcher for truth, operating in a cramped lab, out of touch with practical realities. In the old view, science was thought to be the pure pursuit of truth with unqualified objectivity, using the experimental method. "Pure pursuit" meant without concern for practical application.

Quite distinct from the scientist was the technologist or inventor, working in a practical setting, giving birth to techniques or machines to do useful jobs. Technology was seen as the practical application of the truths of science to give people greater leverage over nature.

The distinction between science and technology was quite clear. Science sought knowledge of the laws of the universe. Technology sought mastery over nature for human purposes. The scientist sought unsullied truth. The technologist sought to fabricate tools and machines to increase human control.

Few today find such a distinction either useful or believable. The modern scientist depends on technology for his instruments and spins off knowledge which spawns new technologies in a systematic manner. A chemist, for example, normally works with a sizeable research staff. The staff run experiments systematically, using expensive centrifuges, microscopes, and computers. The chief chemist is more a manager than an experimenter. Part of the chemist's challenge is to keep the lab furnished with state-of-the-art technology to maximize its effectiveness in research and its chances for success in competition with other laboratories. The results of experimentation are promptly reported and, it is hoped, efficiently adapted for practical advances in medicine, industrial processes, or other applications.

We should discard the older image of technology. It shrouds the actual situation of the contemporary professional. We shall do better to think of a vast scientific-technological complex (sci-tech complex, for short). As Stephen R. Graubard (1980, p. v.), editor of the American Academy of Arts and Sciences, has said in some recent thinking on this issue:

> Too many of us still tend, however unwittingly, to think and write about technology in terms more appropriate to the nineteenth century than to the twentieth, emphasizing the mechanical and the entrepreneurial to the disadvantage of the systemic. A better definition of modern technology insists that it be thought of not as a collection of artifacts, however sophisticated and complex, but *as a system whose social, cultural, intellectual, managerial, and political components are seen as integral to it.*

The sci-tech complex involves not only the scientist who depends on technology for his experimental tools, but includes the social scientist who relies on calculators, computers, and communications devices. It continues with the technologist, who invents new systems, tools, and techniques, adapting scientific discoveries as they become available. It continues through an extensive network of business, government, and educational organizations that raise revenues to invest in research and development and purchase the products. It extends further through the human service professions that adapt and use new technologies in their practices. And it ends with the client or consumer, bedazzled by the cornucopia of medicines, machines, and other modern miracles, but also intimidated by the expertise of those who make them work. This sci-tech system seems to command our lives, even as we acknowledge and help to sustain its influence over us. It permeates the actual working situation for the professions today.

A necessary part of the picture of technology is an understanding of its relationship to geography and culture. Historically, technology has been a human product, not particularly a Western product. Asians, Africans, and Middle Easterners all have heritages of metallurgy, stonework, and practical design. A Persian rug, the Zimbabwe ruins in South-Central Africa—these are examples of marvelous traditional techniques. This is important to note because Western observers have often slighted the traditional technologies of non-Western lands.

Nonetheless, the sci-tech complex in the modern sense is primarily a product of the West—of Europe and North America. One could not have anticipated this modern development in classical times, despite Greek temples, Roman aqueducts, and the mechanical contrivances built by Hero of Alexandria in the second century B.C. One might have had some clue to this future development in the slow accumulation of improved agricultural techniques and sailing vessels in the late medieval era. The proliferation of inventions, such as the timepiece, and practical scientific education flourished in Europe following the Renaissance and the Reformation (fourteenth to sixteenth centuries). But inescapable evidence of European origins of the sci-tech complex came very late, at the end of the eighteenth century, when the steam engine was coupled to productive machines, releasing enormous sources of inanimate power for processing materials such as cotton and laying foundations for the explosive growth of new industry, the development of scientific medicine, and the mechanization of warfare.

Though the modern sci-tech complex is a product of Western

history, culture, and circumstances, the impact has been world-wide. Superior transportation meant going farther from Europe in trade for raw materials as well as in missionary ventures for converts to Christianity. Commercial firms and Christian missions in Asia and Africa demanded European political intervention to ensure their security. Once set up, colonial administrations required increasing tax revenues, so elements of the sci-tech complex, including professionals to operate it, were brought out to speed up the economy. Some host societies gained access to the secrets of the sci-tech complex more quickly than others. Technology was quickly imported, improved, and adapted for local purposes. Japan was a classic instance. In other cases, the colonies were milked, profits were sent home to Europe, and colonial dependency set in.

At present the sci-tech complex has spread worldwide, however unevenly. Some societies are intensively technologized, particularly the Western one-third of the world, including Russia and Japan. Even less technologically developed societies in Asia, Africa, and Latin America are nonetheless severely impacted by the consequences of the sci-tech revolution. In fact, for many Africans, Asians, and Latin Americans, modern technology has an oppressive face, being totally entwined with colonialism and neocolonialism. During the colonial era the technology was managed by expatriates, and information and profits repatriated. In the current era of postindependence, technology is still purchased abroad, which tends to perpetuate economic dependence. Peoples of the Third World have had to fight for access to technology, to university education, and for professional control. Sci-tech is viewed by them as necessary for true independence and human dignity but is almost impossible to attain under present conditions of control.

When considering technology and culture we need to attend to their relationships to religion. Religious faith and the sci-tech complex interact at the two main levels of worldviews and ethics. A professional who is both religiously inclined and technologically proficient will have some sorting out to do at both levels. In one sense science and religious faith are in agreement; they both seek truth, and truth is one. However, their presuppositions and methods tend to diverge. Religious faith, particularly Christian, holds that the universe is an expression of God's creativity and that God's nature is ultimately mysterious to even the most devout soul. The way to ultimate truth is through the contemplation of the mystery of God, which leads to an ethic of service. Scientific worldviews hold that the universe is accessible to human reason, unaided by faith. The way to truth is through experimental observation of reality available to the senses, leading to positive knowledge and an ethic of mastery, prediction, and control.

Competition between positivist science and religious vision has marred the relationship between mystery and mastery for some time. The church rejected Galileo and Copernicus; Darwin, Comte, and Marx rejected religious faith, and so, by and large, have the armies of professionals manning the modern sci-tech complex. Their dream has been that science and technology would provide the basis for and the hope of the evolution of society into higher powers of prediction and control. The way of mystery seems old-fashioned and impractical. However, the repeated failure of science and technology to deliver on that dream has led to disillusionment. Nuclear weapons and environmental deterioration are examples of the failure. Many still hope for some sort of technological fix to solve the problems of the world, but everywhere one sees signs of readiness for a return to traditional sources of guidance. The self-evident authority of the sci-tech complex has become less clear. The chance for dialogue is increasing and a synthesis of mystery and mastery might emerge (See Muelder, 1980).

Earlier it was suggested that an *ethic of enablement* is appropriate to the professions. Now it is appropriate to specify ways in which that ethic, enriched by religious insight, might apply to the problems raised by technology. Enablement in this context suggests that technology be developed and applied *instrumentally,* and not just for its own sake. In other words, just because a certain technology seems possible does not justify the decision to develop it. Instead, the decision could be approached by asking whether the technology, so far as can be foreseen, will aid individual clients, consumer groups, society at large, and the natural environment to attain higher levels of actualization. Religious worldviews would add that control for its own sake is not an end to be sought. Rather, all human work, including that of technological development, ought to proceed in awe-ful recognition of the mystery of ongoing creation of the universe in which professionals are privileged to share.

TECHNOLOGY AND THE SHAPING OF THE PROFESSIONS

The sci-tech complex is even more closely entwined with professions than yet suggested. Professional practices and responsibilities worldwide are drastically affected by one's proximity and access to relevant technologies. We have already seen that both the sci-tech complex and the professions are children of a common parent, the Western tradition. And further, once birthed, they tended to maintain, sustain, and develop each other. The sci-tech complex and professions have been, by and large, coproductive.

At a leading university medical center, infants born quite prematurely are sustained in a high-technology intensive care unit. Automatic devices record and display heartbeat and respiration rates as well as temperature. Respirators deliver warm, moistened air. Tubes feed intravenously. The cradle rocks automatically to simulate the movements of a mother's womb.

This suggests the role of professionals as producers of their technologies, for many of the innovative devices in this neonatal care unit were conceived of by the highly dedicated and skilled nurses and physical therapists who staff the center. Professionals in many fields play active roles in the production of technologies specific to their fields.

Entire professions have grown up with the invention, development, and application of technology as their main service. As already suggested, research scientists are expected to produce practical results. In addition, all of the engineering professions and especially design engineering are expressly devoted to technological development. While these professions have so far reached their highest state of skill in the U.S., the techniques have spread, and in Japan the state-of-the-art seems to be outpacing that in the land of its origin.

Though professionals often recognize their own inventive role, they may not be fully aware of the ways in which technology alters, shapes, and reinvents their very practices. Professions once noted for the human dimension of their service now tend to conform more to technological requirements and nomenclatures. For instance, the "old-fashioned" clergy who still minister in person to gathered congregations are outclassed by television preachers ministering to thousands spread across a far-flung network. Complex machines intervene between nurses, therapists, physicians, and their patients. Managers must alter their ways of communication and adapt to new paperless, electronic technologies. Professional practice in some fields can be viewed almost as a consequence, rather than a cause, of technological development.

More important still are the ways in which technology has altered the very shape and status of the professions. One of the important features of modern society, with its underlying structure of high technology, is the increase in social scale. More and more persons relate to each other in interactions of higher and higher density. This means that professionals often find themselves working in large organizational settings. It also means that the professional organizations themselves are developing into larger, more effective organizations. The skills needed by the professional seeking to work for constructive social purposes in large-scale organizations may be quite different from those acquired through professional training.

Some of the important implications of the increase in technological factors and the technological shaping of the professions are these:

- *Political power.* Professions, through becoming more effectively organized, can wield increasing political power through legislative consultations and lobbying.

- *Economic power.* The specialization of knowledge requiring longer and more scientifically-oriented training creates a scarce and more controlled supply of services, translating into increased economic clout. Professional strikes become public emergencies.

- *Race/sex discrimination.* Though professions are now formally open to persons of all races and to women, the white-male dominance is likely to be maintained as long as women and minorities cannot generally achieve the required levels of technical and scientific skill.

- *Occupational standing.* As a rule, the more closely a profession is wedded to technology, the more highly ranked and rewarded its members. Some professions gain, others lose in the shake-out. Overall, professions probably gain on the rest of society.

- *Dehumanization.* The professional practitioner becomes the manipulator of objects, a reader of printouts, and a master of scientific technique, turning clients into the main objects of manipulation rather than sustaining them through warm human relationships.

Technology has been actively birthed by the professions, but the parents themselves are undergoing rebirth via the metallic-electronic womb of the child. The professions as we have known them, some more drastically than others, are conforming to the criteria of the technological era. The sensitive professional who seeks the synthesis of mystery and mastery will want to be both technically skilled and able to question the consequences of technology on the profession and on society.

TECHNOLOGY FOR WHAT?

The prodigious development of technology has caused shifts in the kinds and magnitudes of ethical questions facing professionals in their relationships to clients and to society. Questions about this trend raised by an ethically sensitive person would center around one main issue: technology for what? Some way of evaluating technology and of guiding its constructive use in large-scale organizational settings will be part of the necessary skills of the future professional.

"For what?" is a question that has been asked for some time but is not yet sufficiently high on the agendas of either professions or of society at large. How long the question has been raised was recently recalled by Elting Morison, Professor Emeritus of Massachusetts Institute of Technology, a participant in a panel on technological issues convened by the American Academy of Arts and Sciences in 1979. Morison (in Graubard, 1980, p. 17) noted that political constraints and managerial skills, no matter how improved, are not sufficient for guiding the development of technology. Then he stated:

We need some surer sense of the base of operations that we are
working on. That is what Huxley said at the dedication of Johns
Hopkins; that he really did not care how powerful America was in
terms of iron, coal, steel, and all that, the essential question is,
what are you going to do with these things?

High on the agenda of the professions, then, as of society itself,
must be debate about the legitimate goals for technological development and application.

In fact, professionals have always been in danger of exploiting
their expertise. But the technologizing of the professions is raising this danger to unprecedented heights, as a visit to a modern
medical specialist might suggest. A woman who recently undertook a series of such visits observed that the physician, as the
dominant technological overlord, treated the staff like his vassals.
And the lowly patients were the serfs, governed by a whole page
of seemingly arbitrary rules that were neither justified nor evidently related to medicine. The rules and practices might possibly
have been designed to raised efficiency and lower prices, but the
bills suggested that the effective impact was rather to heighten
profit. The physician gave the patient a consultation or two over
a long period of treatment, while nurses performed most of the
specific procedures. The patient's role was to accept treatment,
make payments, and not to ask questions. Interpretation: the
physician has sufficient technological expertise to justify to himself controlling the situation entirely. This is not to say that the
patient did not benefit from the treatment, but only that she
thought herself the object of a sort of tyranny.

The foregoing case is mild. Consider the following, a more
excessive case of seeming professional exploitation over portions
of the captive populations in two major state prisons in two of
the nation's western states.

Two prominent research scientists conducted experiments over
a number of years to determine the effects of x-irradiation on
male reproductive capacity. They applied doses of radiation ranging from small to large to the testes of volunteer prisoners. The
effects were measured by analysis of biopsies and by sperm counts
from the volunteers, who had agreed to undergo vasectomies
prior to release from prison as a condition for their participation
in the research. In one prison, volunteers were paid $100 for

the vasectomy. While the volunteers signed informed consent statements, there would appear to be a serious question as to whether members of a captive population such as state prisoners can give free and enlightened consent, especially in the case of research that involves highly intrusive and dangerous medical procedures such as the ones in question here. The technological-scientific mentality seems to have reduced human beings to the status of experimental subjects solely for the purpose of generating research statistics. The purposes of the scientific-technological complex, however important they might have been, were assumed to justify the procedures and to override considerations of human rights.

The danger to humane practice is that the control of technology by professionals might result in a superior, condescending, or exploitative relationship between professionals and clients or professions and society. But that is only one possibility. It is also possible that the expertise acquired by professionals and the professions could be utilized to increase genuine service. Greater technological skill could result in greater service, if rightly directed. Human liberation and a renewal of the world could ensue, but the issue of the direction of technology raises questions that cannot be solved by technology alone.

In a recent dialogue on this very point (in Graubard, 1980, p. 3), Harvey Brooks, Benjamin Pierce Professor of Technology and Public Policy at Harvard, and Joseph Weizenbaum, Professor of Electrical Engineering and Computer Science at Massachusetts Institute of Technology, pinpointed the issue:

> BROOKS: It seems to me that because technology opens up options, it takes a strong value system to control the choice of options; and so, where technology is disastrous is where it enters a culture or a social situation with a weak value system and very little sense of collective welfare.

> WEIZENBAUM: I would like to endorse what has just been said, especially because I think our culture has a weak value system and little use of collective welfare, and is therefore disastrously vulnerable to technology.

What is needed is technology assessment based on a strong sense of values as an integral aspect of normal professional practice. The inventive engineering and design professions should, it would seem, assess the possible social impacts of new technologies and attempt to evaluate them, just as they already evaluate economic impacts. Of course, the means of control is still at issue. Should society itself regulate invention, possibly through governmental jurisdiction? Or should the play of the free market be allowed to dictate the choice between forms of technological development? But the need for assessment is well established.

Nothing here is intended to suggest an antitechnological stance or to defame the sci-tech complex. The purpose has been to suggest the need to raise questions such as these, which have their source in analyzing technology as used in the professions from the reference point suggested by ethics.

- How can a professional constructively employ technology through his or her practice?

- How can one direct his or her profession toward the constructive management of technology?

CONCLUSION

Enough has already been said to conclude that the sci-tech complex and its allies, the professions, have technological powers available for immense good or harm. Professional ethics should provide a perspective from which a professional can raise value questions leading to the management of technology for constructive purposes. In this brief space, no full system for technological assessment could possibly be proposed. (However, see Brooks, 1980; Ellul, 1964; and Faramelli, 1971.) But the starting point can be suggested: namely, a widespread exploration during the next decade of how an ethic of enablement, a theme indigenous to the professions and also supported by religious and philosophical ideals, can serve to help direct the development and application of technology in professional practice.

References and Suggestions for Further Reading

Brooks, Harvey. 1980. "Technology, Evolution, and Purpose," *Daedalus* 109:1 (Winter), pp. 65-81. This article and the entire issue are eminently worth serious study.

Ellul, Jacques. 1964. *The Technological Society.* New York: Vintage Books. A trenchant comment on the destructive nature of technology.

Faramelli, Norman J. 1971. *Technethics:* Christian Mission in an Age of Technology. New York: Friendship Press. An engineer-theologian gives religious perspectives on technology.

Graubard, Stephen R. 1980a. "Preface to the Issue, 'Modern Technology: Problem or Opportunity?'" *Daedalus* 109:1 (Winter), pp. v-vi.

———, ed. 1980b. "Some Issues of Technology," *Daedalus* 109:1 (Winter), pp. 3-24.

Klemm, Friedrich. 1964. *A History of Western Technology.* Trans. by Dorothea Waley Singer. Cambridge, Mass.: M.I.T. Press. An intriguing, standard, older history.

Kranzberg, Melvin and Carroll W. Pursell, Jr. 1967. *Technology in Western Civilization,* Vols. I and II. New York: Oxford University Press. Comprehensive and detailed.

Muelder, Walter G. 1980. "The New Debate on Faith, Science and the Future," *Andover Newton Quarterly* XX, No. 4 (March): 199-207. Reflections on the faith-science-technology debate centered in the World Council of Churches.

Reiser, Stanley Joel. 1978. *Medicine and the Reign of Technology.* Cambridge: Cambridge University Press. The physician has become the prototype of the technological man. This book spells out the costs and benefits.

World Council of Churches. 1979. "Anticipation," No. 25. Ideological and theological debate about faith and science, with many perspectives represented. See also No. 22 (1976).

Think More About It

1. In what ways has your chosen profession, or one you know well, been changed in the past 20 years by technology?

2. What grounds do you, personally, have for questioning and interpreting the development and deployment of technology, in a profession or in society at large?

3. Are we in danger of being overtaken by our technology?

SIX

Problems of Professionals in Large Organizations

The judges of the superior court in a populous county objected as a body to their being held accountable to the county's new ethics code. Their main objection was that they were already subject to the stringent ethics code of their own profession. Most professionals today are themselves caught in the very situation that our judges sought—successfully—to avoid. They find themselves subject to both the claims of a profession and those of a large-scale institutional employer. Such persons have to decide whether the opportunities of work in an institutional setting outweigh the problems of dual loyalties.

Obviously, significant differences exist between one's profession and the organization or bureaucracy that employs one. The profession is a collegial organization of peers with a horizontal line of authority. The institutional employer is a large-scale social structure peopled by persons of diverse work disciplines, both professional and nonprofessional, and organized with a vertical line of authority. In addition, Reinhold Niebuhr (1932, pp. xi-xii) articulated a profound problem:

> A sharp distinction must be drawn between the moral and social behavior of individuals and of social groups. . . . In every human group there is less reason to guide and to check impulse, less capacity for self-transcendence, less ability to comprehend the needs of others, and therefore more unrestrained

egoism than the individuals, who compose the group, reveal in their personal relationships.

In other words, the moral theme of enablement that we have found to be at the heart of professional ethics is challenged in the large-scale organization in which corporate egoism comes to the fore.

A substantial majority of professionals work in institutional settings. Even historically, lecturers have taught in large universities, lawyers have been retained by institutional clients, engineers have had corporate clients or employers, clergy have served in ecclesiastical hierarchies, and health practitioners have been employed by large hospitals. Today, as law firms grow and group medical practices proliferate, more and more formerly independent professionals are being drawn into large organizations (See Moore, 1970, pp. 187-88).

Finding themselves drawn more and more into bureaucracies, often organized around priorities based on self-interest, how do professionals respond? Some, like our judges, try to practice their profession while rejecting the claims of the bureaucracy. Another common reaction was reported by the dean of the professional division of a university: "Professionals across the board," he noted, "are frustrated because they are finding that they cannot practice ethically, in the system." Feeling as though pushed far enough, many have simply ended their careers and have opted out. Like Sir Thomas More or Martin Luther they have cried out, "Here I stand; I can do no other." The woods of Oregon are said to be populated with such persons seeking simpler lives in which integrity can be more easily maintained.

Still others have concluded that big organizations are here to stay for the foreseeable future. They feel that what is needed is to work effectively in bureaucracies—to manage or to shape the organization so it serves some larger good. They agree with the staff of the Center for Ethics and Social Policy: "If we are really concerned about the quality of our world, we must go beyond individual ethics and develop ways to understand and improve the ethics of organizations" (McCoy, Juergensmeyer, and Twining, 1975, p. 3). Such persons are willing to bear the personal costs of corporate affiliation for the sake of the good they might be able to do or the harm they might be able to forestall. Issues facing such professionals are the ones we shall consider here.

UNDERSTANDING LARGE ORGANIZATIONS AS EMPLOYERS

Fear characterizes the view that many persons hold about large organizations. It is partly an inability to understand big institutions that leads to this response. To further the understanding of such organizations, we shall approach them from the perspective of an institutionally employed professional, inquiring about organizational structures, processes, and substance.

Our first concern is with the *internal structure* of an organization, which suggests a framework for the management of decision making and exercise of power. Every professional needs to know where, in his or her large-scale organization, policy decisions are made. Decisions may be made primarily by the chief executive or, more likely, at various decision centers. Thus the first question to ask is, where are specific decisions actually made? Next, one can ask whether the structure of decision making makes sense in terms of organization goals, social values, and moral criteria.

Wherever decisions are made, they must be communicated up and down the management line of authority and across staff groups. To serve this need, an organizational communications system does or should exist and ethical sensitivity can be structured into it.

Officers of a large commercial bank holding company wondered whether the institution was out of step with the changing personal needs and desires of its employees. In order to provide for a better understanding, management instituted a committee to review the company's social responsibility to employees, as well as customers, shareholders and communities served. Members were drawn from a number of organizational levels and many functional areas. The committee was given the mandate to report on values shifts and to make recommendations to the senior management. Within two years the company had addressed itself more satisfactorily to a number of important internal issues, including employee rights.

Taking the lead in the development of ethically-sensitive organizational communications, as illustrated by our financial institution above, is a live possibility for the professional. If channels already exist to provide an inward and upward flow of information from lower and marginal areas toward the decision-making centers, the problem for the concerned professional is to use them well for processing information relative to ethical dimensions of organizational life. If the channels are not in place, then the problems are to sell the idea of building such channels, and to make them work. Decision-making centers require information about moral values and value shifts to increase the responsibility of the organization. All large organizations, public or private, such as hospitals, educational institutions, government agencies, and publicly held conglomerates, would be wise to adapt or develop procedures like these.

The *external structure* of the organization, our second area of concern, refers to the interfacing between a large organization and its social environment. A key objective for organizations is to pattern relationships between the large organization and its clientele, the government, consumer groups, and other interested publics with a view toward gathering information on the concerns and values of the broader society. As consultant Fred Twining and his colleagues state: "For a company which seeks to be a leader in corporate social responsibility, a comprehensive understanding of shifting social values is critical" (Twining, Donahue, and McCoy, 1978, p. 1). In our view, a "comprehensive understanding" is a valid goal for all large organizations, not just business corporations. Once again an example will help to illustrate the main point:

> Management of the same large bank holding company mentioned before charged the same committee with systematically exploring the needs and concerns of the public in its market area. The committee was to report information and to make recommendations for action to management. Management wanted knowledge of changing social values and guidance in adapting the institution to them.

The result was a heightened awareness of corporate responsibility and a number of new programs to allow the organization to respond to legitimate public needs with integrity.

Professionals need to be aware that size concentrates power and power creates suspicions. Groups in the external social environment are well aware of the propensity of corporate groups to pursue their own egoistic aims, the point made by Reinhold Niebuhr above, at the cost of others' legitimate needs and rights. This means that trust will never be won solely on the basis of a superior communications structure but only by the patient building of a track record that qualifies others' initial distrust through demonstrations of fair play.

The term *organizational processes* speaks *internally* to the issue of whether ethical concerns are, in fact, actually being processed in the ongoing life of the organization. *Externally, process* raises the issue of the organization's dominant style of relationship to each of the important groups in its environment. Without such processing, the best organizational structures would be as dead as a skeleton without flesh and blood.

Internally, a key indicator is whether employees are actively encouraged to raise ethical issues. Does the organization provide for and encourage the use of a forum for internal discussion of issues? Is attention to moral issues on the part of employees counted as a strength in the employee evaluation process? Or, alternatively, is the organization ignoring inquiries and even punishing those who raise questions of ethics? Externally, is the institution secretive and combative or reasonably open and cooperative? Does it recognize the value of debate and consultation concerning its social impact? Is the organization disposed to maintain and expand its points of access to local and global social values and interests, or does it seek to close its gates with a slam in order to retreat behind fortress walls?

Finally, in this very brief survey, we reach the topic of *substance. Substance* refers here to the moral content of an organization's institutional life. If *structure* is like the bottom and banks of the river and *process* is like the flow of the stream, then *substance* is the actual water that flows. *Internally,* several specific issues surface with respect to substance. Among them, one would wish to know whether the special purposes of one's own profession are acknowledged as legitimate within the employing institution. For instance, health workers for major-league sports teams are often under intense pressure to play injured players at substantial risk to further injury, a policy which requires doctors and therapists to put ownership's interests above those of their patients. Again, are employees respected as persons? Are rewards and punishments distributed fairly? Are responsibilities assumed for the continuing development of employee skills and abilities?

Externally the issue of substance raises questions about how the organization understands its contributions and responsibilities to society. Does it accept responsibilities that are appropriately balanced with the rights it claims? Of course, virtually all organizations portray themselves as contributors to the public interest or common good in some particular way, such as by producing goods or services. But in practice sometimes the stated benefit is window dressing, hiding an organization's actual highest purpose, which might likely be something like single-minded pursuit of power or wealth.

In sum, the professional employed by a large institution is blessed with the opportunity to work for organizational justice and ethical responsibility. Through seeking ways to promote fairness in organizational life, professional enablers can, through institutional structures, processes, and substance, distribute widely the humane values that form the theme of professional life.

ORGANIZATIONAL ETHICS CODES AND COMMITTEES

Major organizations of all kinds, including both private corporations and public agencies, are adopting with greater frequency ethics or conduct codes. These codes, of course, are in addition to legal charters and applicable laws and regulations. Organizational ethics codes address the issues of the values, loyalties, and rights which the institution expects from its employees or promises to them.

Organizational ethics codes bear a marked superficial resemblance to professional ethics codes, but their implications for the professional are different. The differences are sufficiently significant to warrant our giving considerable attention to them as a separate topic. We shall seek to understand organizational ethics codes and procedures in relationship to the organization itself, to the ethics of professions, and finally to broader ethical principles.

The howl of protest let out by the superior court judges, noted in the opening pages of this chapter, helps to define the difference between professional and organizational ethics codes. Whether judges work for state, city, or federal government, they are governed by the same professional code. Professional codes of ethics define the moral obligations of members of particular professions. Organizational codes, in contrast, set out the moral obligations of the employees of particular bureaucracies, whether business corporations, governments, or not-for-profit service agencies. Such codes apply to all the employees of the organization, nonprofessional and professional alike. How such organizational codes of ethics could help or hinder one's professional vocation becomes a matter of significant concern for all professionals, just as it did for our superior court judges.

In the mid 1970s the employees of the Weyerhaeuser Company, a multibusiness forest products firm, were formally introduced to the existence of their corporate conduct code and Business Conduct Committee. Because this firm began its corporate ethics program somewhat earlier than most, its procedures are more fully developed and therefore can well serve as our primary example. However, we shall also make reference to the codes and procedures of other private and public agencies. The Weyerhaeuser code, printed in a pamphlet of about 6000 words, is of moderate length. Others range from very short (as brief as one paragraph) to long (like a medium-sized book). The Weyerhaeuser pamphlet bears the title, "Weyerhaeuser's Reputation— A Shared Responsibility."

Structural issues, as with professional codes, noted in Chapter 4, include such considerations as: who writes the code, for what audience, and with what authority? The primary responsibility for authorship may lie, as in Weyerhaeuser, with a committee chosen from lower to upper management. By contrast, some other codes are the direct product of the chief executive office. The main question to ask here from the perspective of fair play is whether the structure of the writing process allows for sufficient input from the groups that will be held accountable. When a chief executive, for example, unilaterally dictates an organizational code, some injustice may be done to those who are expected to adhere to it.

For whom is the code written? The target group actually addressed may be different than the stated audience. One experienced observer uses the following rule of thumb: the more voluminous the material, the more likely the real audience is external (government, consumers) rather than internal. Another test is to ask, to whom is the code distributed? In the Weyerhaeuser case, as in many other business examples, all new and continuing salaried employees are targeted. In many research organizations each researcher is informed, as all new research proposals must conform to the code. In other cases the code may never be systematically distributed. Or sometimes the recipients targeted are stockholders, clients, government officials, or whomever the management believes it must reassure about the supposedly high ethical standards of the organization. The point is to be able to distinguish between codes that are intended to be implemented and those that are mere window dressing.

Still speaking of structure, another question is, what authority stands behind the code? In Weyerhaeuser the top management appears to be firmly in support of the code. The corporate president wrote the introduction, for instance, commending the pamphlet in which the code is printed. In other cases boards of directors have considered and supported their codes. For members of the organization to know that they are to take the code seriously, it is essential that legitimate authorities know the code, approve of it, and communicate their support of it.

Turning to the *substance* of the codes, what are their purposes? Caution is in order. Some codes are written mainly to heighten employee loyalty to the organization or to maximize economic performance. This may bring organizational codes into conflict with professional codes and religious or philosophical ethics.

Does the organization subscribe to a legitimate purpose related to a broader vision of life, or does it elevate itself as the world's highest value? Are the purpose(s) of the organization in tension or outright conflict with those of certain professions? As Moore points out, for instance, research professionals want to share the excitement of novel discoveries, but if the professional is working on an invention, she or he may be constrained by the organization to withhold information until the invention is patented (Moore, 1970, p. 204). This is a tension that can be lived with. But if, as in the Nazi case, the implicit purpose of the organization is human exploitation and that of the profession is human

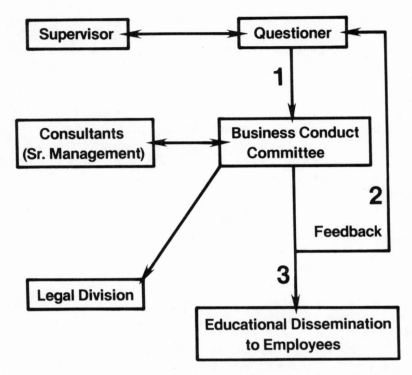

Figure 4. Simplified chart of ethical disclosure and consultation procedures employed in the Weyerhaeuser Company.

health or welfare, the tension may become unbearable.The recent instances of profit-oriented corporations marketing infant formula in Third World nations in allegedly harmful ways seem to fall somewhere between our previous two examples and should have occasioned serious reflection by employees such as managers and nutritionists (See Clement, 1978).

The protection of the good name of the organization often becomes a chief concern of the code. In our major example the title, "Weyerhaeuser's Reputation—A Shared Responsibility," illustrates the point. But a legitimate concern for protection of a good name can and often does shade over the elevation of the company itself as the primary value of employees. When this happens, questions must be raised. Professionals may feel pressured to give an improperly high degree of loyalty to the organization itself, possibly to the extent of compromising their loyalties to other values in their lives. This danger can be illustrated by the CBS Inc. "Guidelines on Business Conduct and Responsibilities" (published in 1976, quoted by permission), which reads:

> The good name of any corporation, as well as its reputation in the marketplace, ultimately depends on the way it conducts its business and the way the public perceives that conduct. . . . No CBS employee should be, or even *seem* to be, subject to influences, interests or relationships which conflict with the best interests of the company.

This could be a morally outrageous statement. If the phrase "the best interests of the company" is narrowly interpreted, then the code seems not to allow for proper balance between corporate and familial, professional, and religious loyalties in the life of its employees. The CBS code seems to illustrate the point made by Courtney C. Murray, former Dean of the Graduate School of Business Administration at Columbia University, when he said, "There is something in the corporation which creates loyalty beyond a healthy condition" (Quoted by Francis, 1979, p. 10).[1]

Whenever an organization, public or private, profit or not-for-profit, seeks to capture its employees' exclusive allegiance, then it only endangers itself. It endangers itself by depriving itself of gains to be realized through internal discussion of corporate abuses. Many an employee has refrained from raising legitimate questions in the corporate forum for fear he might be misconstrued as disloyal. Legitimate and important issues have been papered over; later, costly scandals have erupted.

A preferable alternative is to recognize that every person lives with multiple claims of loyalty. Organizations should provide channels for the debate that will arise when people seek respon-

---

1. Reprinted by permission from *The Christian Science Monitor,* © 1979 The Christian Science Publishing Society. All rights reserved.

sibly to balance their loyalties. As a longtime respected scholar of organizational ethics says, "Management needs to provide its employees with a *reasonable* right of dissent. At the heart of the matter is the balancing of the ethical rights of the individual and the ethical rights of the organization" (Purcell, 1975, p. 47).

A relatively sophisticated balance has been achieved in the Weyerhaeuser code we have been examining. The company recognizes that employees' obligations go beyond narrowly defined corporate interests. For instance, in a concluding section, the code asks employees to consider, "Does this act meet my own personal code of behavior?" Such a question allows for the possibility that employees may find an action compatible with the company interests but in conflict with their own standards. In such a case, the employee could discuss the issue through the normal channels. A likely possibility is that deficiencies in organizational standards would be identified and could be addressed, saving the organization a lot of trouble later on.

Turning, in the third place, to the issue of how organizations *process* their codes and issues that arise, one wants to know how the organization disseminates the code, how it is implemented, and whether discussion of its provisions is actively promoted. Some corporations have developed very advanced dissemination techniques. A large bank not only mailed out its code of conduct to each employee but sponsored small-group discussions of the code, led by selected supervisors. Each employee participated in one such discussion. Hospitals sponsor "ethics rounds" in which cases are discussed in relation to relevant codes. In another case the employees of a large multinational were asked to verify in writing that they had read and understood the code. Parenthetically, professional organizations stand to learn much about effective code implementation from the examples of the most advanced corporations. Code implementation by professions is primitive in comparison.

Corporate conduct committees have become important to code implementation. Again, Weyerhaeuser can serve as an example. When employees formulate questions about ethical matters, it is expected that they will raise the questions with their supervisors. The supervisors answer the questions, if possible, or refer them to appropriate levels in the organization. The Business

Conduct Committee meets regularly to entertain questions and provide counsel on such matters.

Suppose a manager were to become aware of a possible ethical issue related to the allowable degree of social contact between himself and an employee of a competitor company. Our manager wonders whether business conduct principles were being breached. Following the established Weyerhaeuser procedure, his first step would be to consult with his superior about the problem, and they might be able to reach their own determination. If they could reach no firm conclusion, then they would refer the question to the Business Conduct Committee at corporate headquarters. The committee might feel competent to resolve the issue itself or, depending on the implications, might wish to discuss it with senior management or a representative of the legal division. Within three weeks of the initial referral the committee would formulate a reply and send it back to the manager and his supervisor.

The Weyerhaeuser procedures emphasize disclosure. In contrast, a majority of codes stress proscription, what one must not do, or prescription, what one must do. A disclosure code is written in relatively general terms and is designed to provoke questions. Counsel is made available to help answer the questions that arise. In this way a history of cases and judgments accumulates to serve as guides to action.

The organization using the disclosure model obviously places a relatively heavy emphasis on the good judgment and character of its employees. Simultaneously it avoids writing a new Ten Commandments, Hammurabi's Code, or Book of Leviticus for corporate life, in which things to be done and others to be left undone are all spelled out in the form of detailed rules. The organization using the disclosure model says to its staff in effect: "Here are guidelines to point you in the direction of moral behavior. Don't think of them as rules as much as consciousness-raisers. When questions come up, let's discuss them." To give a complete picture we must add parenthetically that legalistic compliance manuals are necessary in addition to disclosure-model codes in those areas and levels of the business in which regulatory and legal controls are particularly significant.

So far we have considered only the dynamics of code processing internal to the organization, but external processes are important too. One of the sources of pressure on organizations to formulate codes and implement them is government, whose task it is to safeguard the common good. When the chairman of the Securities and Exchange Commission emphasizes in speeches the need for higher levels of corporate accountability and suggests that this could be achieved through "accountability boards" and alert board committees, publicly registered organizations of all types sit up and take note. When Ralph Nader calls for committees to protect employee rights, corporations may both cry with indignation and also take note. So external criticism of large organizations is integral to the process of code implementation and undoubtedly has been a major factor in making organizations ready to give the issue a degree of priority in their affairs.

We have described the process, substance, and structure of organizational ethics and have identified some issues raised particularly for professionals. Let us turn now to a different sort of question, namely, how do these codes and procedures fare when evaluated by external norms? We are moving now from mainly descriptive to normative analysis.

First, most organizational codes, like most professional ones, seem to rely very heavily on rule-ethics and pay too little attention to ethics of aspiration and character ethics. If organizations would give more attention to character, the entire range of ethics would be more adequately utilized.

Second, the issue of organizational goals should be more adequately addressed. Many organizations focus on one narrow goal (often increased profit). Restricted focus seems to produce clarity and management control. Yet, the supposed clarity is imaginary and misplaced unless organizational purposes are formulated in terms of the essential values contributed by the institution to society as a whole. Efficient, profitable operation is one such value, but safe and durable products, excellence of services, and employee development are others.

One can rightfully ask of an organization that it conform to a pattern of justice and fair play. Are its returns commensurate with its contributions? Is it concerned with the justice of access to opportunities and benefits it offers? Is it working toward a sustainable society? These are matters that should be the concerns of each major organization and its professional members.

STRATEGIES FOR PROFESSIONAL ENABLERS IN LARGE ORGANIZATIONS

After surveying the risks and pitfalls of working within large organizations, some professionals may choose to drop out, like those mentioned in the introduction to this chapter. Others will decide to continue within the organization to remain an active part of what is the most important experiment of this era of history: how to control large organizations and direct them toward humane and just action. That David prevailed over Goliath and pygmies master elephants should be encouraging to the latter group.

Assuming that one wishes to work within large-scale organizations, what strategies can the professional use? Strategies must be carefully tailored to fit each situation, but the following ideas should be widely applicable.

First, many professionals, like lawyers, physicians, nurses, and therapists, serve in staff positions. Such a position often allows one to give information and advice directly to management for use in decision making. (Persons in line positions, by contrast, mainly carry out directives.) A strategy (if not an obligation) for staff professionals is to call attention to the ethical dimensions of issues under consideration. This may call for clear and courageous statements of views at times.

Second, the provisions of an ethics code and a conduct committee are now widely accepted in organizations of all sorts. If one works in an organization without such structures, an obvious strategy would be to work for their establishment, using the precedents already established by leading organizations across the nation. In pursuing these goals, one can argue very persuasively that the best interests of the organization will be served.

Third, professionals should work toward getting their own professional organizations to provide tangible forms of support for members whose positions are in jeopardy for upholding the ethical principles of the profession. Support can take several forms, ranging from arbitration on the member's behalf with the employing organization to financial support to media exposure of the problem. Each of these forms of support has its own risk level, which must be carefully assessed and weighed before proceeding. The Industrial Designers Society of America and some other engineering professional groups have developed such techniques and seem to be the leaders in this field.

Finally, one may work toward the establishment of voluntary policing groups that transcend particular organizations. An example already established is the National Advertising Review Board. This organization consists of 50 members, 30 representing advertisers, 10 representing ad agencies, and 10 representing the public. It reviews complaints about the truth and accuracy of ads. Additional bodies such as this will surely come into being, especially in industry groups, where the need seems greatest, partly as a result of the urging of the Securities and Exchange Commission. Working from within for voluntary policing is a legitimate, potentially effective strategy.

CONCLUSION

We began this chapter by acknowledging that professionals often react to large organizations with despair and resignation. One can understand why, after considering the facts that go along with bureaucracy and grate against the humane values held by many professionals. In addition, organizational ethics codes and procedures, such as may exist, are quite distinct from professional ethics. They have different purposes and may embody contrasting values. Simultaneous loyalty to both sets of ethics, as well as to the other values in one's life, may entail conflict, even of a serious nature. Yet, professional values can enrich organizations. Also, the control of improvement of large organizations may yet be possible. Professionals, with their special skills and their access to the flow of information in the organization, have important roles to play in initiating improved organizational ethics. These factors support those choosing to stay with the struggle instead of dropping out.

To this point in the book we have sketched the components of professional ethics and have examined its contemporary setting, concentrating on the technological and bureaucratic features of our era. We shall devote the remainder of the book, save the final chapter, to a study of specific issues that arise in professional practice.

References and Suggestions for Further Reading

Clement, D. 1978. "Nestle's Latest Killing in the Bottle-Baby Market." *Business and Society Review* 27 (Summer) : pp. 60-64. One of the many articles that have examined the Nestle case.

Eisenstadt, S. N. 1966. *Modernization: Protest and Change.* Englewood Cliffs, N.J.: Prentice-Hall, Inc. A durable, concise statement of organizational changes in the modern era.

Francis, David R. 1979. "Balancing Profits and Business Ethics." *The Christian Science Monitor*, November 20, p. 10.

Kuhn, James W. 1977. "Socially Responsible Business: Its Past and Future." *Church and Society* LXVII, No. 4 (March-April), pp. 5-11. Eloquent statement of the need for accountability in large corporations.

McCoy, Charles S., Mark Juergensmeyer and Fred Twining. 1975. "Ethics in the Corporate Policy Process: An Introduction." Berkeley: Center for Ethics and Social Policy. A concise introduction to organizational ethics as practiced in one cutting-edge California bank.

Moore, Wilbert E. 1970. *The Professions: Roles and Rules.* New York: Russell Sage Foundation.

Murphy, Catherine P. 1978. "The Moral Situation in Nursing," in E. L. and B. Bandman, eds., *Bioethics and Human Rights.* Boston: Little, Brown, pp. 313-320.

Niebuhr, Reinhold. 1960. *Moral Man and Immoral Society: A Study in Ethics and Politics.* Orig. publ. 1932; New York: Charles Scribner's Sons. A classic theological reflection on the ethical features of large groups.

Purcell, Theodore V. 1975. "A Practical Guide to Ethics in Business." *Business and Society Review* XII (Spring) : pp. 43-51. Toward a balance of employee and organizational rights.

Twining, Fred, Jim Donahue and Charles McCoy. 1978. "Social Value Systems Analysis." Berkeley: Center for Ethics and Social Policy. On institutionalizing corporate social responsibility.

Veatch, Robert M. 1977. "Hospital Ethics Committees: Is There a Role?" *Hastings Center Reports* VII, No. 3 (June) : pp. 22-25.

Think More About It

1. If professions generally were to follow the lead of engineering and adopt procedures to protect their members against employers' actions when the employee seeks to uphold the professional ethics code, how could the professions be prevented from misusing this power for merely self-serving purposes?

2. Organizational ethics codes, as we have learned, are typically rule-bound. What kinds of changes might be proposed to provide for more emphasis on employee responsibility growing out of mature character, and how could such changes be initiated?

3. To what degree can the employee of a large organization effectively articulate challenges on ethical grounds to establish policies and procedures? Apply your answer to this question to a large organization with which you are quite familiar.

PART THREE

ISSUES
IN
PROFESSIONAL ETHICS

SEVEN

Those Near at Hand: Clients

Client relationships give rise to many difficult ethical issues for professionals. The term *client* itself presents some difficulties, because the client may be a single individual in some professions such as many medical fields. For other professions the client may be a group or even a nation (consider the "client" of public health and the military). In business management, law, and the clergy, the client may be a corporate body or an individual person, depending upon the circumstances. Despite these differences, client relationships are a major source of ethical dilemmas for all professionals.

A sixty-year-old patient was referred by Dr. Jones to Allied Physical Therapy Clinic, a private, for-profit organization situated in a large urban hospital. Dr. Jones was a member of the hospital's medical staff. He prescribed ultrasound therapy, a common technique in contemporary P.T. practice. The client was referred to Erika Johnson, a new young staff member at the P.T. clinic, who thought of herself as a competent P.T. and was anxious to gain recognition in the hospital and the clinic for the quality of her work. In the preparatory interview with the patient Erika learned that he had been treated for a carcinoma four years earlier. The carcinoma had been treated with radiation therapy, and no signs of active malignancy had been found in follow-up examinations. Nevertheless, Erika was troubled. She had learned that ultrasound should not be used on patients with a history of cancer because the treatment might possibly disperse a malignancy, and the passage of four years of time was insufficient to guarantee that the cancer was truly "gone." It could merely be in remission and could begin to spread again at any time. She felt caught between her obligation to treat in accordance with the physicians' prescription and her other obligation to serve the patient's best interests.

This case reveals many aspects of professional ethics, so many, in fact, that we can discuss only a few of them. Among those aspects are the changes introduced into professional ethics by technology. Specifically, though ultrasound as a therapeutic technique has been available for about 20 years, its principles and contraindications are not understood by all physicians. Prior to the introduction of ultrasound, this particular problem would not have emerged.

Another aspect is that differences may develop between members of various professional groups over the proper procedure in a particular case. Some of these differences may have little to do with ethics, as such, but may simply represent uneven levels of knowledge or variations in the prevailing norms and interests of different professions. In a medical case, the physician, the nurse, the social worker, and the hospital administrator may well have very different objectives, to say nothing of the third-party payer, the insurance company. In a business situation, the legal department may have a very different outlook on a proposed corporate policy or procedure than the managers in the personnel department. It is prudent for all persons on a professional team working on a problem or case to state their overall perspective, interests, and understanding of key terms.

Instead of spending further time on aspects of the case such as these, we shall concentrate instead on analyzing the options open to Erika Johnson, using this occasion to review and test some of the major types of ethics introduced in Chapter 3.

CLIENTS AND CONSEQUENCES

Erika immediately realized that she needed time to think before deciding what to do to resolve her dilemma. She completed her normal preliminary interview, then gave the client an appointment for a second session in two days. By this means she gained time, always desirable for persons confronting dilemmas, but unfortunately not always available.

During the next two days Erika pondered what to do. Did she have her facts right? She was quickly able to confirm that ultrasound was thought to be capable of dispersing a malignancy. As to the diagnosis, she could get no firm data without going to the physician's file on the patient. She felt that she could not do this because the physician was known to be very authoritative in working with subordinates and might regard such a request as an unwarranted intrusion into the physician's prerogative to prescribe. So she was limited to the client's own remarks.

Next, she tried to detail her other alternatives. She had already decided against warning the physician. The possible consequences for her working relationship with Dr. Jones, and perhaps other physicians, seemed too grave. But she also decided against giving ultrasound therapy on the grounds that there was a chance of harm to the patient.

She continued to explore alternate resolutions to her dilemma. She considered whether to appeal for assistance to the supervisor of the P.T. Clinic, but she decided against this on the grounds that such an action might unnecessarily jeopardize her just-commencing career in that her supervisor might think she lacked self-confidence or the competence to make her own decisions.

In the end, Erika hit upon the seemingly ingenious solution of giving the ultrasound treatment as prescribed but without turning on the machine. In this way, she thought, everyone would be happy: the physician, because treatment seemed to have been administered, and the patient, because treatment seemed to have been received. She faked the ultrasound treatment.

A neutral observer of Erika's approach to this case would have to make several comments. First, a more thorough consequentialist would not have been able to give full approval to Erika's resolution of her dilemma. Reason: she did not consider the consequences for a sufficiently large circle. Nineteenth-century utilitarians said, "Seek the greatest happiness for the greatest number." In contrast, Erika did not, for example, consider the harmful consequences for the insurance company, which would be billed for treatments not given. Surely this would have to be entered as a harmful result. Nor did she consider the possibility that her deceptive act might be discovered, entailing negative consequences for herself, the clinic, the hospital, and perhaps even her entire profession.

Another point would concern the difficulty of making judgments about the ratio of good and bad consequences of an action when the future is unpredictable. Prediction was difficult for Erika in this case, in the first place, because she could not obtain the necessary medical background on the patient to sufficiently understand his history or the reason for the physician's prescription. Her difficulty was made greater by the fact that she had to make guesses about the probable responses of her supervisor and the physician to any inquiries she might have wished to make to them about how to handle the case. Her judgment that she might jeopardize her reputation with them could have been more a reflection of her own fears than a realistic estimate of their probable responses, but in any case she was obviously dealing with probabilities. Thus, in general, one of the weaknesses of utilitarian ethics is the problem of unanticipatable consequences of actions. For this reason, many have been led to judge right and wrong actions on the basis of principle rather than on that of consequences.

DECIDING ON PRINCIPLE

Supposing that Erika had used a rules-ethic approach, would she have been led to a different resolution of the problem? She would have wanted to consider several basic principles, which would have included truth-telling and justice. These principles could be derived from both the deontological ethics of Immanuel Kant and the rich and older natural law ethics traditional to Roman Catholic thought.

Did Erika violate the principle, "Always tell the truth"? Some might argue that she did not lie to the patient, the physician, and her supervisor; she merely did not tell them the full truth of the situation, namely that she used the ultrasound device with the power off. This argument would be difficult to uphold with respect to the insurance company, however, because she had to complete a treatment voucher on which she positively indicated that she had given an ultrasound treatment. One would normally judge this to mean with the power on. With regard to not telling the full truth to the patient, the physician, and her supervisor, it is true that persons often omit telling the entire truth for apparently good reasons. You may ask how your friend is feeling, but your friend may withhold part of the truth to avoid spoiling your morning. This is regarded as civility, not lying. Nevertheless, her decision to withhold part of the truth was made for a consequentialist reason and could not be justified from the perspective of the ethics of obligation. Therefore it seems highly probable that deontologists would judge that Erika had an obligation to inform even the patient, the physician, and the supervisor about her decision not to use ultrasound with the power on.

What about justice? This is an additional principle that might be advanced by the ethics of obligation. In our earlier discussion of deontological ethics in Chapter 3 we did not elaborate the concept of justice; nevertheless, we have been using it synonymously with "fair play." This is a good point at which to introduce a deontological concept of justice in more detail. The principle of *justice* could be understood as *the obligation to give each party its due*, with *due* being *the assignment of costs and benefits that a rational and disinterested observer would make.* Whether the obligation to do justice be grounded in reason, natural law, or religious faith, the emphasis falls on doing justice because it is right.

Applying this understanding of justice to the ultrasound case reveals some new considerations. Particularly important is the fact that the insurance company will be unjustly presented with a claim for payment; the claim will be unjust because a disinterested observer would judge that no corresponding benefit was received. Although many people, in actual practice, might have few scruples about presenting a small medical bill like the one we are now considering to a large and probably wealthy financial institution such as an insurance company, and might even consider it to be a clever way of shifting a burden to a giant that can easily bear it, the deontologist would argue that just relationships at all levels of magnitude are essential to a well-ordered society. From this point of view Erika ought to have found a resolution to her dilemma that would have allowed her to avoid perpetrating an injustice on the company.

Yet other principles could be used in clarifying Erika's dilemma, the chief being that clients should be treated as ends in themselves, never as means alone. Erika seems to have used this patient largely as a means to the ends of avoiding conflict with superiors and of safeguarding her own career. Admittedly, she acknowledged the patient's value by not doing anything that might disperse cancer, but this respect for the patient seemed secondary to her own ends, thus leading to the conclusion that she used the patient as a means.

Erika's abridgement of the principle of persons-as-ends-in-themselves, however, was very mild compared to other instances. For example, in Ursula LeGuin's futuristic novel, *The Lathe of Heaven* (1971), the psychologist, Dr. Haber, takes a patient, George Orr, who has the power of dreaming "effectively." By dreaming of another state of being for the world, Orr can actually change history, but instead of desiring to use his power, he wants to be cured of it. However, Dr. Haber, by guiding the dreamer by hypnotic suggestions, tries to use George's power to bring about a utopia free from overpopulation, disease, and war. In his relentless pursuit of this utopia, manipulating George's powers of effective dreaming as his means, the psychologist himself goes mad.

Enough has been said in this brief application of the ethics of obligation to Erika's dilemma to indicate that her way of resolving it raises questions when examined from deontological perspectives. Even if the ethics of obligation do not provide automatic answers, they do bring clarity to the situation. From the point of view of the "ethics of responsibility," the way of moral decision making we settled upon as the most appropriate in our discussion in Chapter 4, attention to principles is part of the art of moral judgment.

EGOISM

We shall take just one more approach to Erika's case in order to further illuminate the issues of client relationships. Recalling our brief introduction of the concept of egoism in Chapter 3, we said that the egoist asks, "How may I act so as to maximize my own greatest long-term benefits?" This is a form, as we said, of the ethics of aspiration, or teleology.

One can notice elements of egoism in Erika's decision-making process. Evidently the course of action that she finally chose was based, in large part, on her decision to act in such a way as to safeguard her position in the clinic and in the hospital and to further her own career aspirations. Apparently she valued her own prospects more than she esteemed fair play and justice. This reading, of course, would be difficult to prove, since motives are private and therefore difficult to discern.

Egoism presents serious difficulties for professionals, and nowhere do they emerge more clearly than in client relationships. First, its very status as an ethic can be denied because it acknowledges no moral obligations to patients and customers, but uses them as means to its own end. In addition, egoism negates the moral theme of enablement that we discovered to be indigenous to the ethics of the professions. Only the professional is enabled, and at the clients' expense! Consequently, an unqualified egoism could never serve as the basis for truly professional client relations.

But let us give Erika credit where credit is due. We must acknowledge that she tempered her concerns for her own career advancement by her unwillingness to commit physical harm to the patient. Caught in a difficult dilemma, she apparently formulated a course of action out of dual concern for both herself and her patient, shifting the costs of the action mainly to the insurance company. On her behalf, then, one must say that she qualified the egoism and apparently sought to decrease the ratio of costs to benefits by shifting the former to a large, impersonal bureaucracy.

In fact, a limited degree of egoism does have a place in ethics. For instance, Jesus counseled, "So whatever you wish that men would do to you, do so to them" (Matthew 7:12), which admits of self-interest at least to the extent of regarding one's own claims in relationship to those of other persons. Further, common sense approaches have long recognized that one has to love oneself before one can love others. So a limited degree of egoism or self-regard, understood in this way, is legitimate.

The problem with egoism as a guide to decision making seems to arise when it is detached from a broader system of loyalties and obligations and one's self is made the supreme value. Egoism in this sense is almost universally condemned. With respect to client relationships, if professionals seek to advance their own interests without offering a reasonable value in terms of goods or services, they have lost sight of mutual obligations and broader loyalties and have allowed egoism to run rampant. This is the classic source of client exploitation.

What should Erika have done? As we have already seen that ethics does not involve an exact calculus, we can only point to a range of several ethically correct alternatives for action. But all of them would revolve around keeping client welfare uppermost and doing justice to the insurer. Bringing the supervisor into the case would certainly be important. Erika would have to decide whether and how to confront the physician on the basis of her self-acknowledged view of legitimate relationships between other members of the health care delivery team and the physician. Moral behavior extends over a range that ends in, but doesn't necessarily require, heroism. Support for whatever alternative she chose could be marshaled from the physical therapy code of ethics and possibly from the hospital ethics committee and from the state or national physical therapy association. Finally, if Erika had chosen to deal with the broader ramifications of the matter, she could have tried to work through her association, hospital, and other available channels to modify the authority relationship that so tightly binds the therapist to the physician, a form of superiority quite difficult to justify on the grounds of justice and superior knowledge. The unjustifiable superiority of the physician in this case is probably the overarching consideration. It seems to have provoked the dilemma and to have biased the therapist-patient relationship to the detriment of the client's health. In conclusion, Erika's decision allowed her to avoid inflicting direct harm on the patient. However, she seems to have been too concerned to conceal from her superior and the physician her legitimate concerns about the dangers of the prescription, probably out of fear for her own career and at the expense of the insurance company. An ethic of responsibility would have counseled a more discerning interpretation of her supervisor's legitimate concerns and of her relationship to the physician, as well as greater regard for the principle of just financial relationships with the insurer.

CONFIDENTIALITY

Many other issues grow out of professional-client relationships. One area fraught with recurring storms of debate is that of the confidentiality of records. Legality aside, which has established benchmark standards in the Family Privacy Act of 1976, what information about clients can be stored and who should have access to it? At what point does lunchtime discussion with colleagues about a patient's medical history, a student's academic deficiencies, a client's legal exposure, or a customer's credit history become unethical? If I store information about a client, am I obligated to disclose the fact of its storage, the nature of the data, and the limits to its use?

Standards in some professions have been very high with regard to confidentiality. Traditionally standards have been highest in the medical and ministerial professions. Since the Oath of Hippocrates, medical practitioners have been bound to protect confidences. The principle, as reaffirmed in the 1949 International Code of Medical Ethics, states, "A doctor shall preserve absolute secrecy on all he knows about his patient because of the confidence entrusted in him." As for the clergy, priests and ministers have always maintained the principle of confidentiality in pastoral relationships. The standards of the legal profession are comparable, as are those of journalism and some law enforcement agencies.

The problematic issues have to do with access to information. For instance, hospital records indicate the nature of the illnesses and the treatment given to patients. Should a researcher studying diseases of the liver be given access to the records of such patients so that he can contact them for information? Should a college professor have access to the prior academic records of his current students in order to determine how best to help them? Should a commercial firm compile and release information concerning its customers' buying habits and/or life-styles?

The urgency of such questions arises partly from technological changes, such as the development of information gathering, storage, and retrieval networks. It also arises from obvious abuses, as when a researcher or salesperson approaches a prospect with an announcement like, "I noticed from our computer printout that you. . . . "

The concern for confidentiality has two sources. One is sheer pragmatism. If ministers discuss their parishioners' confidences, nurses tell their patients' secrets, or journalists divulge their sources, these professions would not long endure. The keeping of confidences is essential to effective professional work.

The second source is the concern for human rights. Privacy is one such right and is held to be particularly important in the American culture. Just where the right to privacy ends and the need for publicity begins is subject to recurring debate; the line will shift over time and in different circumstances. In our culture the right to privacy is currently gaining greater importance. Two working principles would be that confidences must be respected by professionals and not divulged except under legal constraint, and perhaps not even then in certain cases; and that clients should be informed about the contents of stored information and the safeguards regulating its use.

CLIENT AUTONOMY

Another important issue is the autonomy of the client. The underlying ethical principle is the Kantian imperative that persons ought to be treated as ends and not merely as means. We noted some degree of violation of client autonomy in the Erika Johnson case; the problem recurs in many forms.

Client autonomy is an issue that may threaten professionals because it seems to undermine their authority to make decisions that command respect. Many are used to thinking that they are entitled to make decisions unilaterally. Client autonomy suggests that the professional's right to decide is qualified by the patient's responsibility to himself or herself.

We seem to be moving toward a situation in which most professionals will regard their relationship to the client as a partnership in which decision-making authority is shared. If the client is incompetent mentally, then his or her authority should be assumed by a relative or legally appointed guardian. But normally the patient is competent to know the good he or she seeks and comes to the professional for enabling skills and knowledge. The theme of enablement takes full account of this shift toward greater client autonomy and supports it. Whereas the older concept of client service seems to suggest the patient or customer as the passive recipient of professional paternalism, the concept of enablement recognizes that clients have a legitimate right to be informed about their situations and to assist up to the limits of their competence in the selection of services to be rendered or products to be purchased. Under the concept of enablement, responsibility for the course of action chosen is shared between professionals and clients.

To understand the essence of the argument, consider the question that arises in medicine: does the patient have a right to die? The health practitioners' obligation to preserve life is qualified by the patient's right to choose death if his continued life seems the greater of two evils. However, great care must be exercised; the patient's right to autonomy must also be qualified by a number of factors. One such factor, besides that already mentioned of competence, is consistency: is the patient's request to die consistent with that person's history of choices and general dispositions? This test is necessary because persons in need of making such a decision are normally so pressured by the circumstances that judgment is impaired.

CONCLUSION

We discovered that accepted ethical standards for client relations vary from profession to profession and have developed over time. New standards are evolving to meet new conditions brought about through technological development and the modernization of the professions. Although our primary case had its main bearing on the health professions, the general conclusions reached seem equally applicable to adaptation by the entire range of professions within our purview in this book.

A philosophy of client enablement has been assumed and elaborated. According to this, the good of the client should be the professional's primary concern. The client's understanding of the good will normally be presumed to be valid. This principle is based on a notion of personal autonomy of clients as ends-in-themselves. The principle of autonomy must be applied with judgment within the context of other principles, especially that of justice. In deciding in the mode of the ethics of responsibility, application of principles must also be made with regard for the consequences of the proposed action on the client, the institution, and the broader community. The professional is neither a dictator nor a technocrat but an enabler working in the context of trust.

References and Suggestions for Further Reading

Aroskar, Mila Ann. 1980. "Ethics of Nurse-Patient Relationships." *Nurse Educator* (March-April): pp. 18-20. Four models for medical practitioner/patient relationships.

Bourricaud, François. 1979. "Individualistic Mobilization and the Crisis of Professional Authority." *Daedalus* 108 (2): pp. 1-20. The bases of professional authority relative to clients, in the light of threats to the relationship.

Guccione, Andrew A. 1980. "Ethical Issues in Physical Therapy Practice." *Physical Therapy* 60 (10), pp. 1264-1272. A summary of which ethical decisions are most frequently encountered by and most difficult for practicing physical therapists to make.

LeGuin, Ursula K. 1973. *The Lathe of Heaven.* New York: Avon Books. For rethinking client relationships, this novel is very productive of questions and insights.

Robitscher, Jonas B. 1972. "The Right to Die." *Hastings Center Report* 2:4 (September), pp. 11-13.

Think More About It

1. Ask a professional to discuss the greatest ethical dilemma he has faced in relating to a client. What were the circumstances? How does he define the dilemma? How was the dilemma resolved?

2. To what degree can egoism be appropriately or constructively incorporated into a professional's ethical decision making with respect to clients?

3. What rights would you claim as a client? With respect to knowing the full facts of your situation as diagnosed by the professional? To know what records are being kept and with what safeguards?

4. If Dr. Haber had been able to create a utopia on earth using George Orr's power of "effective dreaming," would he have been justified?

EIGHT

Those Near at Hand:
Subordinates, Peers, and Superiors

More and more, professionals find themselves knit into service-delivery teams, working with other professionals and allied workers to bring more comprehensive or specialized skills to bear on the needs of the client. The interdisciplinary team contrasts to the fee-for-service professional who, at one time, might have had an exclusive one-to-one relationship with the client. Such team relationships, of course, are nothing new to the management professions, but for many other professions the new approach greatly complicates the moral situation.

The theme of client relationships, therefore, needs supplementation. Now we need to indicate some of the other moral obligations the professional has as well. Attention must also be given to ethical subordinate, peer, and superior relationships.

SUPERVISING SUBORDINATES

"Nonmanagement professionals" may be surprised to find themselves in supervisory and administrative roles, feel untrained for them, and perhaps unwilling to move out of direct services positions. Nevertheless, nurses, for example, may find themselves in charge of seven to fifteen subordinates not long after beginning their careers. And professors may become deans; parish clergy, judicatory officials; lawyers, managing partners; and so on. The profession most untouched by this trend is that of physicians.

But partnerships, group practices, and health-care teams in hospitals commonly place even the doctor in a quasi-management role.

It is quite amazing how little preparation is given to professionals for their management roles (management professions excepted). Since formal preparation is not normally offered, professionals are left to their own devices for gaining management skills and perspectives. This immediately creates a certain problem for any professional assuming a management role. Psychological and ethical adjustments to the problems of management are difficult when rational preparation has been neglected. One solution is to take short courses in management. These have proliferated in recent years; the quality varies and the students must be selective. Another is to find an experienced manager-professional to act as a mentor.

The primary ethical problems in supervising others, whether they happen to be professionals or not, come in providing subordinates with sufficient freedom to exercise their own responsibility and autonomy while assuming full responsibility for the maintenance of adequate standards. A balance between extremes must be struck by the use of imagination and through plenty of communication.

Judging from conversations with current and prospective supervisors, one of the common extremes into which they unfortunately fall is to condone the subordination of the values of the client or the employing institution to the personal career goals of the members of the service delivery team. This kind of error is illustrated by a testimony from a professional manager in a business corporation:

"I have to get quality work out of the people that work for me," said a mid-management official. "So as soon as they come on board, I tell them in strong terms, 'If you help me look good to my boss, I'll help you get ahead too. But if you don't produce for me, out you go, no questions asked.'"

How does the handling of relationships with subordinates exemplified in this quotation fare when analyzed ethically? One could answer this from a consequentialist point of view by asking: what ends are being sought? It seems clear that the end being sought by the manager is his own career advancement.

He assumes that his subordinates will adopt the same goal for themselves and that their various self-interests are complementary and can be mutually satisfied. Since we have already acknowledged the rightfulness of a degree of self-interest, we cannot suggest here that the career goals of the professional suprvisor and his subordinates should be totally disregarded or nullified. But we can state that to subordinate the good of the client(s) and of the employing institution to one's own career advancement is to fall into almost unqualified egoism.

A balance should be struck between all relevant moral obligations so that the professional team becomes much more than a conspiracy between the members for their own advancement. Recognition of such a balance is given in the following remark by other managers in the same organization as our egoist above. Their message to their subordinates went like this:

> We are trying hard to deliver quality products to our customers, working within the constraints of the marketplace. We want to achieve acceptable ethical standards at the same time. This organization has an important mission to fulfill and we count on your wholehearted cooperation in achieving it.

This approach places the superior-subordinate relationship within the broader context of an organizational mission and standard. The validity of this alternative assumes that the mission referred to is important in terms of human need and the common good.

Professionals as supervisors have an obligation to communicate ethically compelling expectations to subordinates. This means devoting much thought to guidelines and goals and encouraging open communication about them. "Justifiable" in this context means a proper balance between competing legitimate claims and obligations, with the assumption being that client enablement receives first consideration.

Techniques have been developed, some of which are commonsensical and others more imaginative, for achieving both freedom and responsibility in superior-subordinate relations. In addition to those mentioned in Chapter 6, the organizational ethics code, conduct committee, and the goals of disclosure and dialogue, we shall mention two more at this point. First, supervising nurses have particular difficulty in giving both the desirable freedom to the subordinates and also guaranteeing the privacy of their patients' medical records. Medical students and nurses' aides often discuss highly confidential material among themselves, as in the lunchroom, or even in public. Obviously, this poses a danger to patient privacy. Nurses seem to agree that should one learn of a breach of confidentiality, the supervisor must take the subordinate aside, explore the issue, and verify the standards. This straightforward technique seems to meet the criteria of establishing clear standards and communicating them, while still preserving the freedom of the subordinate to do the right.

A more formal approach, also from the field of medical services, is imaginative and deserves attention. The approach is called the "ethics round." A work team including physicians, nurses, and therapists in a certain unit, for instance, sets aside time on a regular basis for discussing the ethical dimensions of particular cases. Ordinarily they will invite a trained ethicist to act as facilitator (See Levine, 1977 and Davis, 1979). This technique and others like it help to build an ethical "culture" within a work group, with a common vocabulary and common goals and values. This technique could be transferred to other settings such as business management, education, and religious organizations.

Whether the "ethics rounds" approach or one of the more structured methods discussed in Chapter 6 should be adopted depends to a large extent on the size of a given unit and the size of the entire organization within which the unit is located. The general goal would be the same—to develop and communicate common expectations and to make ethical behavior a normal part of the superior-subordinate relationship.

Superior-subordinate relationships, to be healthy, must be reciprocal. The problem for the superior is not only to grant subordinates freedom to do the right but also to hold himself or herself accountable to the same standards that he or she expects of others. Supervisors seem to grow used to wielding power over others without acknowledging the right of those they supervise to raise questions about the deportment of the manager.

Obviously, to assert that superiors should be accountable to a degree to those whom they supervise may seem a radical and troubling approach. It raises many questions about proper authority. Generally, authority merely imposed by fiat is fragile; sound authority arises out of mutual responsibility. Structures can be invented to minimize the delicacy of questioning authority, such as ethics rounds that use hypothetical cases and involve both superiors and subordinates in the discussion. Sensitive managers will hear and respond to comments directed at hypothetical behavior analogous to their own. More direct confrontations may also occur, such as in the case of a physician who once heard from an exasperated therapist in the same unit that he had no special moral authority to make certain ethical decisions without consulting others. Though superiors may find it difficult to believe, challenges made by subordinates can be very helpful to the superior and may avert bigger problems at a later time.

In summary, ingenuity and courage are necessary in dealing creatively with the problem of superior-subordinate relations to achieve the goal of recognizing the autonomy of all parties while maintaining legitimate standards.

COLLEAGUES AS PEERS

When one moves from subordinates to colleagues in the same profession, the problem shifts to balancing between the loyalty due to individual members, on the one hand, and simultaneously maintaining the integrity of the entire professional body on the other. By becoming a member of a profession, a person assumes both responsibilities.

What is a peer? A peer is a professional equal, a member of the same or an allied discipline. In the older language, now thankfully relegated to the past, a peer is a member of the "brotherhood." A peer is part competitor, part team player. Peers are bound to each other by common values and constraints. The normal relationship is one of loyalty, teamwork, mutual assistance, and sharing.

Teamwork and mutual assistance are exemplified in many disciplines. Teachers, for instance, frequently and freely share syllabi of their courses in the hope that whatever is of value will be adopted by others for the upgrading of the profession and the good of the students. Researchers share new knowledge through professional meetings and journals, and medical practitioners share techniques. Remarkably, the ethic of sharing and mutual assistance obtains to a large degree even in business relationships, a surprising finding since cutthroat competition is often perceived to be the usual mode of procedure. For instance, a unit in one corporation was very generous in sharing the technical side of its computing techniques with the counterpart unit in a similar business.

Problems in collegial relationships often come to a head when it is discovered that the behavior of one professional endangers the standards or integrity of the body in a significant way. The issue can be delineated by going back to Erika Johnson's situation for a moment. As introduced in Chapter 7, Erika, a physical therapist, faked an ultrasound treatment. If another therapist had discovered that Erika was only pretending to give ultrasound, what should he have done? Following the physical therapy association's code literally, he should have initiated disciplinary proceedings. However, that seems to invoke too strong a measure for the severity of the particular violation. A more responsible course of action would have been to consult with her to find a better resolution to her dilemma.

How can and do professionals respond when they learn that a colleague has fallen into a clear pattern of ethical failure? Sometimes, out of a sense of loyalty, colleagues may close ranks around an individual, protecting the fellow member like wolves an injured member of the pack. The problem with this response is that an injustice may be done to the client or to society out of unchallenged loyalty to the colleague. On the other hand, errant individuals have been shunned in the most petty of ways by, for example, having certain privileges as the key to the executive or physician's washroom removed. Eventually the shunned colleague gets the message and leaves the hospital or the company and may simply go to another vicinity where standards are lower. In this latter case the problem is not resolved but merely transferred to another setting where the public is more defenseless. Costs are assumed by the errant colleague, whose fundamental problem has been overlooked, and by colleagues and clients in the new setting, who may go through months or years of injury until the cycle repeats itself. Somehow a better balance must be found between supporting one's colleague and maintaining the standards of the profession.

More constructive is the approach of informal peer influence:

Engineers in a metals business were becoming more and more concerned about one of their number. His performance at mid-career seemed to be slacking off. He had very nearly ceased attending the professional meetings of his society. Those closest to him observed that he was growing lax, especially in the final testing of products prior to their release for shipment to customers. They talked about this growing concern and decided to handle it informally. A couple of his friends stressed their invitation to accompany them to an engineer meeting, hoping thereby to get him back into dialogue with the profession. The concerned group also delegated two other colleagues to go to him for a chat, in which they gently but openly stated their concerns and asked the man for his feelings and comments.

In this case, a few weeks after launching these low-keyed initiatives, his colleagues noticed that their friend's work was beginning to improve.

Many professions are adopting a requirement for continuing education, partly in response to the growing need for heightened moral consciousness. A requirement for earning a certain number of credits over a limited period of years in order to retain active certification is instituted. Through the means of constant exposure of all of the members to new developments and standards, the problem of maintaining the quality of the profession as well as loyalty to individual members is at least partially resolved. The difficulty with this approach is that the ones most in need of upgrading in a particular area, such as ethics, may be the last to choose continuing education offerings.

Another tactic for dealing with accountability is peer review. This is a decentralized procedure in which the U. S. Department of Health and Human Services, for example, requires each institution which sponsors research involving human subjects to establish an in-house committee to evaluate proposals by both ethical and technical criteria. The existence of the committees and the policies they implement help in keeping research projects up to standard in the planning stage as well as in the implementation phases. If this technique were to be transferred from research institutions into program agencies or business, proposals for changes, such as new projects or expansions of old ones, would be required to pass scrutiny for criteria including ethical standards.

A closely related procedure, commonly practiced in institutions of higher education as well as in some churches, is that of professional evaluation. Normally this involves the preparation of formalized statements by peers, clients, and superiors. The peer evaluations along with the others are then assessed by a group competent to make judgments. Formal evaluation by peers is not normally practiced, to the best of my knowledge, in hierarchical business structures at present, but nevertheless occurs in an informal and therefore often arbitrary way. It is suggested that the more formalized approach could well be more fair, beneficial, and useful than the informal arbitrary approach in business.

In each of these forms of peer assistance to colleagues several dangers must be recognized and acknowledged. First, the evaluation procedures are subject to abuse, as when an irate colleague or a client attempts to impede the career of an individual by submitting a biased or dishonest evaluation. A second, more subtle, danger is that the common standards of any group of peers tend to pull individuals from the edges of the population toward the center. When it results in controlling substandard deviations, this pull toward the center is good. But the problem arises in that very valuable creative behavior may be impeded as well, with the net result that the profession's own progress is retarded through peer control. Persons must be aware of these limitations on the peer-review process and constantly evaluate it to determine whether the net marginal costs outweigh the benefits.

SUPERIORS

The difficulty involved in maintaining ethical relationships to superiors is a feature that is abundantly present for professionals in many types of large organizations. Commenting on findings based on a very thorough survey of business persons regarding management ethics, Brenner and Molander (1977, p. 60) state:

> We feel it particularly noteworthy that relations with superiors are the primary category of ethical conflict. Respondents frequently complained of superiors' pressure to support incorrect viewpoints, sign false documents, overlook the ethical violations of superiors' friends.[1]

From the perspective of allied health, Ruth Purtilo (1978, p. 15) reports that, "Perhaps the question of authority and obedience within the medical hierarchy is the overarching moral consideration facing the allied health professional."[1] Interviews with nurses have convinced me that most nurses face grave problems in relating to physicians if they think and speak independently on ethical matters. The problem extends to other professions as well. Even a pastor reported that sacrifices of integrity were necessary to get appointments to the best churches in his denomination.

The widespread difficulty of maintaining ethical relationships with superiors is ironic considering that high-level managers tend to think that the ethical tone of their organization is dependent solely upon their personal example. Particularly with regard to business, both executives and academic observers have maintained that the "better" organizations are kept that way by the high standards maintained at the top. If managers are, in fact, persons of such high ethical standards, then why do subordinates report that the greatest source of moral difficulty for them is in relationships with the boss?

Some cause is operating here that is important to ferret out. On the one hand, superiors are probably well aware of the shakiness of their positions. When they are questioned, their defensiveness may rise out of a fear of losing authority, status, or income. Above all, they do not wish to give subordinates grounds for questioning the legitimacy of their superiors' responsibilities and privileges. On the other hand, subordinates are often resentful of the prerogatives and perquisites of superiors, and some are constantly scanning for deficiencies in behavior or attitude that could be used as justification for gaining for themselves some larger share of the pie. These observations about human relations are to acknowledge that disputes about ethics in superior-subordinate relations may arise from an economic or power base. As long as class and income distinctions separate professional groups from each other and professionals from their one-time colleagues, such factors must be considered in the analysis.

---

1. Reprinted with permission of The Hastings Center. © Institute of Society, Ethics and the Life Sciences, 360 Broadway, Hastings-on-Hudson, N.Y. 10706.

After such factors have been considered, however, subordinates will still often find that their own standards of ethics or those of their professions are jeopardized by demands made by their superiors. A subordinate in such a situation would be wise to develop lateral ties in the organization for protection in case of administrative backlash. This is simply prudent. A series of strategies are possible once the safety net is spread. One is to try discreetly to learn how far the chain of unethical behavior extends up the ladder. If it goes straight to the chief executive office, going over the head of one's superior would be foolish. On the other hand, if the superior's ethics vary from those of higher managers, a discreet revelation of the situation is one possible strategy, but it carries with it risks of retaliation against which no final assurances are possible. Another possibility is a direct confrontation and an exploration of the problem; perhaps the clarification of differing perspectives will lead to agreement.

As an example that subordinates can win their cases when they stand on principle, the story of an accountant in a medium-sized wholesaling firm is assuring. The accountant was approached by his superior to divulge information about one of the firm's customers' financial status—information to which the accountant had privileged access. The accountant refused to give out the requested information on the grounds that it would be unethical, but the superior persisted in his request. The accountant took his case straight to the president of the firm, explaining the request and his reasons for not complying. The president backed the accountant and ordered the superior to stop making such requests.

This example, of course, is not entirely representative. Not all higher managers understand moral argument and act on principle, as did the president of this company. Sometimes the entire system is rotten from the top down, as in the case of Nazi Germany or as the Nixon White House was asserted to be. In such cases, more drastic strategies are required.

Whistle-blowing, or going public with charges against one's organization or superior, is a drastic strategy. It should be reserved for the most extreme cases. Whistle-blowing is very admirable when a person reveals wrongdoing and thereby brings pressure to bear that averts tragedy. Even when the whistle-blower has good cause, is clearly right, and the superiors are clearly wrong, however, he or she may suffer recrimination, including loss of position and blackballing. This warning is not intended to stop whistle-blowing, but rather to point out that ethical behavior is not always rewarded, at least not in this world, and may prove to be quite costly to individuals.

Another far less drastic possibility is to utilize established internal audit and compliance procedures. If the audit committee of the board is comprised of knowledgeable and strong directors, they will have created institutional mechanisms by which to receive information about ethical lapses and will act to correct them.

Still to be considered is action in concert with others rather than as an individual. Collective action by committees of professionals spreads the risk and enhances one's power. Strategies range from quiet negotiation to informational strikes and mass resignations.

A decision-making framework is of great value in ethical reflection when deciding which of the possible strategies to use. What are the factual dimensions of the situation? As stated above, some disagreements with superiors can be resolved if one can determine that facts and not principles are at issue. Another question to resolve is how to interpret the superior's motives and goals. What is he seeking to accomplish? How does he view the moral propriety of his acts? Next, if principles or values are found to be truly at issue, how vital or fundamental are they? If one judges that a grave moral compromise is occurring, one may have to choose one of the stronger strategies and accept the consequences. Finally, what are one's own goals? Specifically, what standards does one wish to maintain and what level of risk or cost is acceptable? Realistically, the costs of challenging superiors can be grim.

A word should be said here about the term *confrontation,* used so frequently in the past few pages. Confrontation may be sought simply to clarify a situation or to examine its implications. As used in this chapter it is a helpful action intended to bring another to possibly more acceptable levels of behavior.

Confrontations are frequently occasions for fear and defensiveness, since an element of threat may be present. One may not be able to anticipate the intentions of the other party, or one may have good reason to be wary. However, if pursued in the manner suggested here, confrontation can often clear the air and lead to improved, rather than to worsened, relationships.

In confrontations, one should:

- state clearly the purpose of the conversation,
- avoid attacks on persons,
- suggest the benefits to clients and other relevant parties of alternative standards or procedures,
- conclude by summarizing one's position or complaints and restating the desired changes.

THE PROFESSIONAL IN THE MIDDLE

It should be clear by now that some of the most painful professional problems of an ethical nature are the result of conflicting obligations to clients, on the one hand, and to employing institutions or supervisors, on the other. This is the problem of the "professional in the middle." Erika Johnson's dilemma arose precisely because she had one obligation to the physician and another conflicting obligation to the client. Similar cases are easily imagined. Should university teachers strike, as they have done, even though students are deprived temporarily of instruction? Should nurses or physicians strike, leaving patients without medical care?

The problem surfaces in its most acute form when the client and the employer are not the same person. Fee-for-service professionals do not normally face this particular problem because their "employers" are their clients. Physicians in hospitals and chief executive officers may not face intensely the problem of the professional in the middle because their high positions in their institutions tend to free them from accountability to still higher officials. Nurses, therapists, social workers, certain middle managers, teachers, clergy, and accountants belong to the professions where this problem reaches its most critical form (See Jameton, 1977).

The problem in these cases is not normally how to avoid evil and do good. The issue is generally rather how to choose between doing two competing goods or between mitigating two evils. If I act so as to stem one evil, I necessarily commit another or, if I act to do one good, I must leave another undone.

No entirely satisfactory resolution of such cases is available. Each must be weighed on its merits, the appropriate action taken, and the consequences accepted. When the situation is recognized and acted on, a person can take pride in saying, "I've done my best."

CONCLUSION

The professional is usually obligated not only to the patient or customer but to others as well. Multiple obligations can lead to moral conflicts which must be sorted out responsibly in the situation. Responsible ethical reflection is the necessary basis for dealing with the varied and possibly critical challenges that one might face. No entirely satisfactory resolution may be attainable in every situation. Realistically one has to do one's best and be prepared to accept less than perfect solutions.

In exploring relationships with those near at hand to professionals, we have been aware that more distant organizations, governments, and society in general also loom large as sources of ethical standards, challenges, and obligations. Beginning first with governmental relations in Chapter 9 and moving to yet broader social issues in Chapter 10, we shall be changing our emphasis from personal to social ethics as applied to professional practice.

References and Suggestions for Further Reading

Brenner, Steven N. and Earl A. Molander. 1977. "Is the Ethics of Business Changing?" *Harvard Business Review* LV (1): pp. 57-71.

Davis, Anne J. 1979. "Ethics Rounds with Intensive Care Nurses." *Nursing Clinics of North America* 14:1 (March): pp. 45-55.

Jameton, Andrew. 1977. "The Nurse: When Roles and Rules Conflict." *Hastings Center Report* (August): pp. 22-23.

Levine, Melvin D., Lee Scott, and William J. Curran. 1977. "Ethics Rounds in a Childrens' Medical Center: Evaluation of a Hospital-Based Program for Continuing Education in Medical Ethics." *Pediatrics* 60: pp. 202-208.

Purtilo, Ruth B. 1978. "Ethics Teaching in Allied Health Fields." *Hastings Center Report* (April): pp. 14-15.

Think More About It

1. Are measures for dealing with ethical problems related to superiors better developed (less poorly developed?) in nursing and allied health or business?

2. Is a professional group ever justified in striking? For what reasons? Would certain strike strategies be more acceptable than others?

3. An industrial chemist complains, "My supervisor continually asks me to enter false figures in the quality-control records for government contracts. We deliver subquality jet fuel, but the records always are to show shipments as meeting or exceeding minimum specifications." What factors should this chemist consider?

NINE

Government and the Professions: Partnership or Struggle for Dominance?

"Get government off our backs!" was the rallying cry of Ronald Reagan's successful presidential campaign in 1980. Undoubtedly professionals were among the many who responded positively to this indignant protest against government controls. An ethical review, however, suggests that governmental controls over professional activity are justifiable to a degree.

THE STATE OF
GOVERNMENTAL–PROFESSIONAL
INTERACTION

In a legally complex society such as the U.S., many professions depend on legislation for their existence. Of course, the legal foundation varies depending upon the profession and the state or jurisdiction in question.

Specifically, the health professions in various states of the U.S. are established legally by practice acts that set out minimum standards and establish areas of competence. Professionals wishing to practice on a permanent basis in a particular state have to qualify for licensure by successfully completing a state-authorized examination. The legal foundation of certified public accounting is similar.

A somewhat different standing is accorded to the legal profession. In this case the standards governing admittance to professional practice are set by the state professional association, the bar. By law, one must pass the bar to act as an attorney. In effect, the state delegates its power of setting standards to the professional organization itself, a fact which seems to enhance the power and prestige of the bar association as compared to that of the various medical professions.

Still other professions are scarcely established by civil law at all. In the U.S., college and university professors, for example, are not state-licensed, unlike elementary and secondary teachers. Likewise, the clergy are free to set their own standards and administer them, state-church separation being the fundamental reason in this case. Management, likewise, is not state-governed, largely because of its minimal development as a profession.

Beyond direct legislation, however, all professions are subject, directly or indirectly, to regulation. This arises when local governments or state or federal legislatures pass acts creating administrative agencies with the rule-making authority over limited areas of competence. Regulations are thus known as "administrative law," and they serve to establish uniform standards for products, services, or procedures.

A limited picture of the dimensions to which regulation has grown in the U.S. would have to include at least the following: the Department of Agriculture, the Environmental Protection Agency, the Federal Trade Commission, the Food and Drug Administration, the Occupational Safety and Health Administration of the Department of Labor, the National Labor Relations Board, the Securities and Exchange Commission, and the Internal Revenue Service. In addition to these eight, many other federal agencies are heavily involved in regulation, and we have not even attempted an overview of state agencies. According to one report (Malone, 1980, p. 9),

> The federal government now has 58 regulatory agencies that each year issue about 7,000 rules and policy statements, 2,000 of which are legally binding. Of these, the White House reports that 150 have major economic effects. The estimated cost of meeting new health, safety, and environmental standards: $100 billion to $150 billion a year.[1]

---

1. Reprinted by permission from *The Christian Science Monitor*, © 1980 The Christian Science Publishing Society. All rights reserved.

Given the sheer bulk of regulation, it is hardly surprising that professionals and the lay public are reacting with cries of pain. Add to this bulk the overlap, lack of coordination, and occasional contradiction between regulations of various agencies at both federal and state levels, and one begins to understand the reasons underlying people's agony. Bear in mind also that each regulatory agency has some form of sanctioning power, ranging from the levying of small fines to very large ones, the revocation of permits, the withdrawal of government contracts, to applying criminal and civil penalties. The situation has become such that even officials in regulatory agencies are complaining of requirements imposed on them for submitting proposed regulations to multiple bureaus for review and approval. It takes too long to get the new "regs" printed!

It is important to stand back from the whole scene of governmental control of professions and of organizations in which professionals work to ask some questions of ethical significance.

WHY AND HOW
REGULATORY MEASURES ORIGINATE

Two important factors have led to the rise of regulation in our day. The first factor, a very general one, is the complexity of the social, economic, and technological civilization in which we live. Such expertise, such detailed knowledge, is required to understand the complicated changes taking place that administrative agencies with specialized staffs have become a necessity for adequate governance. The rise of the professions, as we have seen, is part and parcel of modern complexity, and therefore of the total milieu which gives rise to regulation.

Abuse of the public's trust, however, is the specific cause of most regulation. The typical pattern begins with the discovery of a significant abuse of professional or organizational prerogatives. The pattern can be illustrated by reference to the regulation of medical research on human subjects.

This story begins with the exploitation of human beings for medical research in German concentration and prisoner-of-war camps under the Nazi regime. After the Allied victory, war crimes trials were held at Nuremberg to assess responsibility and to mete out justice for the horrors. (Some of this story was told in Chapter 1.) Upon the conclusion of the trials, in which a substantial number of professionals were found guilty, the tribunal wrote the Nuremberg Code, a series of principles to govern medical research. Among other matters the Code stipulated that medical research involving human beings must not be carried out without their voluntary consent or in circumstances in which disabling injury can be reasonably anticipated. A cost-benefit rule was also established by which the anticipated good results must justify the performance of the research.

The disclosures of the Nuremberg trials alerted professionals and the lay public around the world to the grave dangers of the misuse of professional privileges. Several consequences occurred that figure into our story. For one, the World Medical Association developed the Declaration of Helsinki, adopted in final form in 1964. This code incorporated the basic principles of the Nuremberg Code in a more refined and elaborate form. The Helsinki Declaration made it clear that research, if carried out in combination with professional care, must be justified by its therapeutic value for the patient. In nontherapeutic research the doctor must still remain the protector of the life and health of the subject. In addition the subject must be in such a state as to be able to exercise fully the freedom of choice implied by "informed" consent.

Somewhat later in the decade, a large agency of a state in the American West—an agency responsible for the administration of the state's prisons—set up a research review committee to oversee research in administrative, technical, and ethical respects. (This case was introduced in Chapter 5.) The committee's first task was to identify and review all ongoing research. In the course of this, it was discovered that a large experiment was being conducted by a prestigious researcher on inmates of the state's major prison (a similar experiment was being conducted by another researcher in a second western state). The review committee wished to know the details and investigated further into the case.

Only after much effort, involving records searches, telephone calls, and telegrams, did the administrators of the research review committee learn the dimensions of the experiment. In very brief outline, the researcher was applying x-irradiation to the testes of prisoners to determine its effect on sperm production. The range of doses ran from seven rads to four hundred. Each prisoner involved in the study had signed a voluntary consent form, and the researcher had also taped oral consent statements. In addition, two research review committees of the researcher's home university had examined the research plan and approved it. One of the committees approved it on both technical and moral grounds. Further, the agency research review committee members learned that prisoner research was sponsored by the Atomic Energy Commission. The A.E.C.'s precise interest in the experiment was never determined by my informant but was assumed to involve the setting of radiation exposure standards for workers in the industry. An additional feature of the research was that the prisoners volunteering for research participation had to agree to undergo lateral vasectomies after research and prior to release. Prisoners were paid a stipend ranging from five to twenty dollars per month during the research and one hundred dollars for undergoing the vasectomy.

The review committee, which at that time consisted of five members, took the position that the research was in gross violation of human rights and had to be stopped. However, obstacles remained, including the fact that the chief administrator of the agency saw nothing wrong with the research. By dint of forceful argument, including appeal to the Nuremberg Code and other statements of ethics, the committee finally prevailed, and the research was ordered halted.

Even though most of the parties involved in deciding the fate of this experimentation defended it technically and ethically, serious questions and objections could be raised against it. On behalf of the continuation of the experiment, the researcher pointed out that comparable information could not be obtained by using animal subjects and that society would benefit greatly by learning more about the critical dosage of radiation necessary for causing infertility. Against the experiments are numerous other arguments. Among them, first, is the issue of subject selection: why were prisoners, and not others, chosen? Undoubtedly they were chosen simply for purposes of convenience and willingness, leading to the conclusion that an injustice was done to them since they had to bear great risks while others would benefit. Second is the matter of benevolence: was it the intent of the experimenter to benefit his subjects in any way?

Aside from the small monthly stipend each received, no other benefit was evident. Although still other objections could be raised, we shall mention lastly the issue of informed consent. Were the subjects informed, in language they could understand, of all the risks? And even if they were, was it possible for them, as prisoners and therefore subject to a coercive situation, to give their consent freely? (See National Commission, 1978, for examples of such reasoning.)

Most independent and objective observers today would surely conclude that the conditions of the use of prisoners as subjects in this experimentation were unjustifiable and extremely offensive and that the research review board of the state agency was definitely correct in ordering the procedure stopped. Because those most directly involved, however, such as the primary researcher and his two committees of reference at his university, were blind to these arguments, outside regulators had to step in to govern the situation. In like manner history has shown that industrialists may be insensitive to the pollutants their plants release into the atmosphere and water, food producers to the toxic ingredients in their products, and automobile manufacturers to the safety hazards connected with the operation of their cars.

Back to the example, an amazing confirmation of the insight and courage of the new research review committee occurred several years later when the A.E.C. gave way to the Energy Research and Development Agency. E.R.D.A. employees, in searching A.E.C. files, discovered records of the prisoner radiation experiment and apparently leaked them to the press in Washington, D.C. The news was flashed by wire and within hours the governors of the states in which the research had been conducted, who had never heard of the experiment, were queried by the local press. Very shortly, in the state in which the agency responsible for prisons had established a review committee, a representative of the governor was in the office of the review committee to get details for the governor. Once informed, the governor and the press were satisfied with the committee's actions which had, years earlier, led to the discontinuation of the research.

A final link in the story is that in 1980 the Food and Drug Administration of the Department of Health and Human Services issued new regulations to take effect in 1981 for the protection of prisoners used as subjects in research. The regulations embodied criteria used earlier by the state agency committee, including the rule that the research must have the intent and probable effect of improving the health and well-being of the subjects themselves (See Federal Register, Book 1, May 30, 1980, "Rules and Regulations").

This brief vignette illustrates much about the growth of regulation. First, an abuse was identified, but recognized only by a very few, who had to stand against the majority opinion of review boards, administrators, and researchers of equal technical competence. Only years later had public values developed to the point that a majority would recognize the radiation experiment as an abuse. Why did the agency committee have this insight? Partly because of perspective. The researcher, the A.E.C., and the university review committees all had a vested interest in seeing the research continue, but that interest was not shared by the agency committee. Personal biography was another factor: one of the review committee members had been close to the events which led to the Nuremberg trials and had a deep personal interest in the applicability of the Nuremberg Code to the ethics of the radiation research being conducted in the state's prison.

Second, public ethical standards evolved over time: the climate changed, and regulatory mechanisms and rules were developed in response.

Why, then, does regulation occur? Largely, to put a stop to what comes to be perceived as an abuse. This is true in the professions and in business. Illegal corporate gifts during the 1972 presidential campaign led to regulations regarding public disclosures. Overseas sales bribes led to the Foreign Corrupt Practices Act of 1977. Inordinate capital expenditures by hospitals in competition for patients led to local health resource planning committees. Alleged abuses of Medicare and Medicaid programs led to review boards to stop such practices. Campaigning against competition among physicians by the A.M.A. led the Federal Trade Commission to ban "ethical" restrictions on advertising of fees and other information by doctors. And on it goes.

Finally, do regulatory mechanisms and measures have a legitimate moral basis? It is difficult to conclude otherwise. Regulation is a major means to make professionals and large organizations in which professionals work accountable to the public and to evolving standards of conduct. However, as already noted, regulation has considerable costs, ambiguities, and limitations that suggest the need for a continuing surveillance of the regulators themselves, lest they get carried away by singular and narrow-minded devotion to their own special form of activity—rule making.

PROFESSIONAL CIVIC RESPONSIBILITIES

Probably it can be agreed that professionals and professions have two sorts of responsibilities with respect to the body politic. One sort is to act within the law, including regulations. A second and complementary sort of responsibility is to fulfill civic responsibilities that go beyond the law. Such responsibilities would include identifying clearly their own chief service(s) and providing the same with high standards of performance. The civic responsibilities would also include managing the large organizations for which they may be responsible according to emerging standards and public values. This will provide the most effective guard against further regulation. Self-regulation can preempt the need for legislation.

Civic responsibilities also include constructive political activity in areas of competence, particularly by supplying relevant information to lawmakers as revisions are being made to the governing legal and regulatory framework. As an example, one midwestern industrial corporation which has come under heavy regulation in recent years has taken a conciliatory and cooperative stance toward regulators working together to devise rules that protect parties all around. Officials of the corporation claim that the results please all parties.

Finally, as a part of their civic responsibility, professions and professionals have a duty to tend and nurture the *general political process* by which issues are surfaced, debated, and resolved in American life. This could mean any number of things, including ably representing positions on issues in the public debate, spending part of one's career in public office, supporting worthy candidates for office, and opposing political corruption. Professionals should look for ways to be effectively involved in political life, because a degenerate political system will make it impossible for professions to carry out their own special tasks in a worthy manner.

Again, the Holocaust and the Nazi period in general is fruitful for thinking about this. We have already observed that professionals of virtually all sorts participated in and supported the Nazi war effort. That effort and the Auschwitz horrors in particular would probably have been impossible without the involvement of professionals.

In their own defense, some of those charged with crimes replied that they had no choice, they were acting under the orders of superiors, and they had no power to stop the experiments. These reasons mean that the political climate, the law, and regulations in Germany had degenerated to the point that professionals were forced to act altogether contrary to their enabling mission. But the question naturally arises, will other professions in other times and places act earlier to nip political disintegration before it flowers so hideously as to require a war to stop it?

Cases can be found in which professionals have arisen to stop the general disintegration of a nation. In 1977 two powerful professions, law and medicine, joined forces in a strike to force a corrupt military regime to agree to return the nation of Ghana to civilian rule. For six months doctors and lawyers withheld their services while the government utilized harassment tactics to put down the opposition. Now, this action raises serious moral questions. Professionals are obligated in principle to supply their services to those in need. Did circumstances in Ghana justify excepting themselves from this principle? Second, were Ghanaian professionals justified in using a bad means (withholding services) to reach a good end (political revitalization)? Third, were the personal costs of lost income, reputation, and continuous harassment worth the ultimate victory? The point, however, is still clear that a precedent was set for constructive political action by professionals and professions.

In the U.S., however, such clear cases do not spring to mind. In fact, the entire Watergate episode raised very serious questions about the resolve of professions and professionals to give of themselves to oppose corruption and nurture good government. Watergate presents the spectacle of certain legal and political professionals intentionally plunging this nation into grave political crisis. The president and those surrounding him were primarily lawyers, and financing for his 1972 campaign was reportedly obtained in part from illegal contributions by American corporations and manufacturing groups.

Did any professional bodies oppose the rot? Not the clergy, nor the professors, nor medical groups, as bodies. Not even the journalists, who were perhaps closest of all to the facts. In fairness it must be acknowledged that the A.B.A. issued a statement very late in the episode accusing the president of trying to "abort the established processes of law" (Ben-Veniste, 1977, p. 150).

Still more, of course, needs to be said. Individual business leaders, clergy, and professors did make clear statements of warning and opposition. Two or three newspapers and a handful of journalists dug out and published the facts, enduring scathing denunciations and elaborate discrediting schemes from politicians. And finally, several lawyers, some acting as administrators of the Department of Justice, others as prosecutors, and yet others as elected representatives, were instrumental in bringing the episode to a worthy close.

But the overall pattern remains one of failure to take timely action. And it is because of this that professions in America, and elsewhere too, need to carefully consider the dimensions of their civic responsibilities. But this requires a theory of government, and too few have such a theory.

A THEORY OF PROFESSIONAL–GOVERNMENTAL INTERACTION

In order to justify many of the positions taken in the foregoing, a theory of professional-governmental interaction will have to be briefly sketched. The leading concept for a viable theory incorporating the best of our rich heritage is that of a people united into a commonwealth or a covenant community devoted to the common good. The concept has deep roots in American history, as reference to the full titles of two of our earliest-founded states, the Commonwealths of Massachusetts and Virginia, will suggest. The basic idea, following John Winthrop and others, is that of a people, a body, or a community united around common values, meanings, and sentiments.

Within this community, work is divided but the separate

tasks are for the common good. Hence, government has for its chief task the achievement of liberty and justice, and each commercial organization contributes its own specific services or products. Thus, for example, manufacturers produce goods to satisfy material needs of food, shelter, and transportation. Medical professions promote health. Electronic communications industries are devoted to creation, storage, and exchange of information, but each for the common good.

Still within the broad picture are the professions, each providing its own special services. Because of its devotion to do its own work in cooperation with society, each profession can be considered as a little government unto itself. Each is responsible for keeping its own house in order and for pursuing its own end or goal. Self-regulation, therefore, is the ideal. What is needed is personal and professional responsibility, not just more law.

But it is apparent that the ideal is rarely reached, and to rest an entire theory of government-professional interaction on an unattained ideal might be naive. One must also take cognizance of the power of self-interest in human life. As John Locke and Thomas Hobbes point out, persons grasp for private property. And in "the city of man," as Augustine suggests, cupidity or selfishness reigns. Niebuhr reminds us that this is especially true of large groups.

Hence, government and law come into play, not just as guarantors of freedom and justice, but as restraints against evil. A historic function of law and regulation has been to curb the undue self-seeking of individuals and organizations. Realistically this function may grow in importance in our economic civilizaton, in which the pursuit of self-interest is stimulated perhaps even more than in other settings. In contemporary language, law and regulation can be understood as our society's imposition of a bottom floor below which no group or person will be allowed to sink without penalty. In other words, since no group or person can be trusted totally to do the right, an accountability mechanism must be structured into society, and that is law.

We have, then, a commonwealth bound by common meanings in devotion to the good. This is the dominant note. The subdominant theme is a realistic view of human self-interest and the need to guard the commonwealth against its rise.

The great tragedy is that at this time the community of meaning seems to have been drained to a large extent out of the life of professions, commercial organizations, and government. As a panelist on a television program devoted to the economy dourly stated, "Human greed is the greatest factor running the economy." Under such circumstances the issue is, who can be trusted? As if to substantiate the panelist's point, business and professional scandals seem to be matched about equally by those of government. Since people can not be assumed to do the right thing spontaneously, the bottom floor of law and regulation has to be moved higher and higher if the level of public ethics is to rise. This is a chief factor leading to the unfortunate necessity of increasing legalism of American life and to the proliferation of regulations that govern professional action.

CONCLUSION

What is needed is less to "get government off our backs" than to renew our classical culture of the commonwealth and the covenant. Science and technology, professional knowledge and expertise must be set within this context. Failing this the future of governmental-professional interaction would seem to be one of increasing conflict, of competition for dominance and control. But given this renewal, a way beyond increasing competition toward a more cooperative society of responsible parties can be foreseen. Our society could become more of an association of persons in community, exercising mutual responsibility, pursuing enhanced social and personal development.

References and Suggestions for Further Reading

Committee on Corporate Law, American Bar Association. 1978. "A Guide to the New Section 13 (6) (2) Accounting Requirements of the Securities Exchanges, October of 1934 (Section 102 of the Foreign Corrupt Practices Act of 1977.)" *The Business Lawyer,* Vol. 34, No. 1 (November), pp. 5-23. A thorough analysis of the impact of one new law on accounting, legal, and management practice.

Bellah, Robert N. 1975. *The Broken Covenant: American Civil Religion in Time of Trial.* New York: Seabury Press. A guide to the commonwealth-covenant theory of government.

Ben-Veniste, R. and G. Frampton, Jr. 1977. *Stonewall.* New York: Simon & Schuster.

Brown, Courtney C. 1979. *Beyond the Bottom Line.* New York: Mac-Millan. Suggestions for internal and social accountability of business.

Clinard, Marshall B., *et. al.* 1979. *Illegal Corporate Behavior.* Washington, D.C.: U.S. Department of Justice; National Institute of Law Enforcement and Criminal Justice. A large-scale investigation of governmental regulation and corporate violations.

Malone, Julia. 1980. "When the Courts Invade the Board Room," *The Christian Science Monitor* (October 9), pp. 1, 9.

National Commission for the Protection of Human Subject of Biomedical and Behavioral Research. 1978. "The Belmont Report: Ethical Principles and Guidelines for the Protection of Human Subjects of Research." Washington, D.C.: U.S. Government Printing Office.

Think More About It

1. What is the legal and regulatory framework of your profession? Is this framework morally justifiable in your view? Why or why not?

2. Did the impetus for the regulation of your profession arise mainly out of an abuse of public trust, or was some other factor more important?

3. Do professionals you know view their civic responsibilities along the lines pictured in this chapter? If so, do they actually act on their views?

TEN

Professional Responsibility
in the Broader World

Shouldn't professionals be aware of long-range trends in the world? Shouldn't they also, through their professions, work for constructive change in the broader world? It would seem unsatisfactory to discuss professional ethics today without pointing to such worldwide issues as malnutrition and the energy crisis. Because of the increase in social scale, most professionals are entwined in a global network by virtue of their work. It is not just that many professionals will be based abroad for part or all of their working lives in, for example, the Peace Corps, the armed services, temporary contract work, or permanent positions in multinational organizations. Nor is it just that professional organizations are beginning to link up in transnational federations in which global problems and standards are discussed; the International Nursing Association and the World Medical Association are examples. It is also that events and forces originating abroad may affect one's work and well-being at home. Thus, having begun with studies of relationships with those near at hand and proceeded through intermediate levels of interaction, we now arrive at the broadest social context of professional practice, the global environment.

FACTORS IN THE GLOBAL SITUATION

The most essential point to recognize is that nations are, and will continue through this century to be, working out of the colonial era and dealing with its lingering implications. Colonialism is a situation in which one nation is dependent on another for direction in politics, economics, and culture. Much of Asia and almost all of Africa was politically and economically subordinate to European colonial powers during the nineteenth and twentieth centuries. Since World War II about 100 nations on these continents have achieved political independence. But enormous economic problems still remain for most of them, as well as for much of Latin America. From the perspective of these developing nations, economic development and securing control of their own destinies are the main issues, and roadblocks consist of the practices and arrangements of Western nations and multinational corporations that seem to conspire against their progress. The liberation sought by developing nations presents challenges in the professional fields of law, health, governmental relations, business, education, science, technology, and religion. The process through which redress is sought has been referred to as the North-South Dialogue. Because professionals have been identified historically with the more developed nations, this struggle for release from dependency greatly heightens the possibility that, in developing nations, professionals will be assumed to be exploitative until contrary evidence is provided.

Another important factor is that, through the increase in social scale, multiple value systems and cultural viewpoints may be encountered within a single organization. A large corporation or international agency will be troubled by cultural pluralism. In addition, practicing professionals may serve clients in other locales with radically dissimilar viewpoints. For instance, increased profit margins may not always be regarded as good, nor may increased rates of efficiency. Medicine may be viewed more as magic than as science. In such ways, cultural pluralism frequently challenges the assumptions on which professional practice and large organizations are based.

A third point is the recent proliferation of multinational organizations. Such organizations are not new, as attested by the Roman Empire, the Islamic empires, the Roman Catholic Church, and ancient trading companies. However, since World War II, they have increased both in number and influence. Contemporary multinational organizations include the United Nations and many other international agencies, churches, and business corporations. Cultural pluralism exists by definition in these organizations, and they are the setting for much of the North-South Dialogue, which might well be understood as an intense, though slightly muted, conflict over the distribution of the world's wealth and political power.

With these general factors in the world situation resting in the background, let us turn to a consideration of several issues to which professionals could give concentrated attention. The stance in this chapter is that it is better to engage the issues than to ignore them, even if one must be selective in focusing on just one of the great array of urgent problems.

POPULATION

The growth in the size of the human population in the post-colonial era has been staggering. In 1953 there were roughly 2.7 billion, in 1978 about 4 billion, and by the year 2000 there will be between 6 and 7 billion people on earth. It is in Asia, Latin America, and Africa that great increases are occurring—precisely in those lands in which Third World issues are paramount and technology is new. It is significant that the current phase of population growth is the second within relatively recent history; during the Industrial Era the European population, now nearly stabilized, underwent a similar burst in growth.

The services of professionals have contributed to the burgeoning of the human population. By researching and developing public health measures, they have contributed to the lowering of mortality rates. Such measures, while good in themselves, have brought harmful, though unintended, consequences, because other measures necessary to support growing populations were not taken at the appropriate times. At this point, other professions seem to be relevant to this picture by their neglect of concomitant forms of development, such as social security assistance and a variety of cultural and economic measures. Reliable social security would replace a large family as the means of support in old age, and economic development would provide food and jobs for the increasing numbers of young people.

Interpretations of these facts vary drastically, and each position is informed by ethical concerns. We shall survey two positions and suggest a third. First, biologist Garrett Hardin and others have put forward a position known as "life-boat ethics." Arguing with respect to some overpopulated lands that it is against the love principle to give food aid, Hardin believes that controlling population through increasing deaths in the near term will result in the best outcome in the long term. He asserts that too large a population will exceed the earth's limited carrying capacity and, ultimately, even the nations with stable population growth rates, such as our own, will be overwhelmed, and all will be lost.

As a policy position, Hardin's argument invites ethical analysis. One may approve of the love motive to which he appeals, as well as his long-term perspective, and yet disagree with his proposed action by noting that his conclusions depend on a concept of carrying capacity and a projection of future consequences which are highly debatable. The actual carrying capacity of the earth is rated much higher by some scholars than by Hardin, and the giving of food aid to nations with high population growth rates may not necessarily contribute to further population growth. Psychological and economic factors play a part in determining the fertility rate, as well as the availability of food. Finally, one might disagree when Hardin suggests that protecting the carrying capacity is a higher ethical principle than the sanctity of life. Both are of great importance and must be pursued together.

An alternate analysis is provided by spokespersons for Third World nations and their supporters, who frequently make two points. One, the issue is not necessarily, anyway, that of population alone, but rather of population in interaction with the rates at which food and natural resources are consumed. They point out that one American devastates the environment at his standard of living as much as ten peasants at theirs. Second, the drive emanating from European lands to control population growth worldwide is viewed by many as a means of retaining world power through keeping non-European and non-North American populations from expanding to their natural levels. These analysts conclude by calling for a reduction in rates of consumption by Western lands coupled with a redistribution of wealth to create conditions in the developing world such that its people will no longer feel compelled to have children as a hedge against economic insecurity. The chief ethical component of this position is an appeal to justice and equity.

Since these two—and other—competing positions exist, each professional, professional association, and large organization willing to respond to the challenge of growing population must weigh the alternatives, come to a conclusion, and adopt an action plan that makes sense in the light of its unique circumstances. The great danger is that people will feel overwhelmed by the magnitude and the complexity of the issue and therefore do nothing. Of course, no one person or organization can solve the problem alone. But each can do something, even if just a little, toward its resolution.

Here are examples of concrete proposals for action that various professional groups, organizations, or individuals might consider. Businesses should examine the justness of the returns they give for services rendered or raw materials supplied in areas of high population growth. They could contribute to food production and housing in local economies. Medical professionals and organizations should address proper nutrition, especially for mothers and children, and the effectiveness of older people in the workplace. Politicians and public managers should give attention to old age security and to removing tax programs that give incentives to large families. These proposals are aimed at insuring people's health and economic security, which should result in controlling population growth by decreasing the number of births rather than increasing the number of deaths. The strategy is to control the size of the human population without violating either the need to protect the carrying capacity of earth or the principle of the sanctity of life.

FOOD, NUTRITION, AND HEALTH

As we have indicated, the rate of population growth is closely tied to food, nutrition, and health. Worldwide, a war on hunger has been declared but is not yet being seriously fought. While per capita food production has been increasing very slowly, the number of malnourished persons has also increased to about 500 million. Many of these are to be found in "food priority countries," so designated by the U. N. because of major recurring food deficits and malnutrition. Malnutrition leads to insufficient human energy for economic development, to brain damage, and to the susceptibility to disease. Most people living in developing nations in tropical areas are subject to debilitating disease and have no access to a physician. To be healthy in such circumstances is exceptional.

How rapidly can food production (and thus nutrition) be increased? Third World nations, represented by the "Group of 77," argue for an increase of 4 percent per capita per year. Western nations and the U.S. in particular argue that this goal is unattainable. Closely connected is the question of how much funding Western nations are willing to put into the international development effort in return for increases in food production.

Yet another question is, how can public health be significantly increased? In poor nations, little money and few facilities are available for research. Wealthy nations have money and facilities for research. Who should decide which priorities should be followed for health research? Similarly, should scarce national health care funds be devoted to high technology medical equipment or to basic public health measures such as clean water supplies? Should one nation be equipping its hospitals with elaborate testing equipment when another nation can hardly afford syringes?

It seems reasonable to urge strongly that professionals in relevant disciplines devote their skills and talents to these complex, interrelated phenomena of food, nutrition, and health with a view toward cutting through the barriers and finding effective remedies. For one reason, professionals are as well equipped as most others to consider carefully the interrelationship of economic and political factors. Equally convincing, professionals, having contributed to the problems, should now contribute also to the solutions.

In this process ethical dimensions should be approached with due consideration. Is the prevention of starvation and malnutrition a defensible short-term goal? Then the apparent means is additional redistribution of food from surplus to deficit areas. Is local or even regional self-sufficiency in food production a justifiable long-term goal? For this, stimulation of agricultural production and land redistribution in food deficit areas may be the appropriate measures. In the realm of health, campaigns against common debilitating diseases that affect many would seem to have higher priority than providing expensive technologies that serve the few at very high cost. Companies involved in selling processed food products in developing nations would seem to have an obligation to make sure, at least, that their products do no substantial harm. None of these remarks is intended to suggest simple solutions to complex problems, but rather to call attention to the need for professionals to debate, decide, and to act to overcome or reduce global nutritional and health problems.

As an example of issues encountered by a world struggling with health priorities and nutritional deficits, the battle over the marketing of infant formulae in Third World nations is instructive. In the mid-1970s, several interest groups opened campaigns against American and Swiss companies marketing infant formulae in developing countries. The interest groups charged that mother's milk was better and that the commercial product was marketed and used in dangerous ways; the companies replied that their product was healthful. Sales techniques were questioned, as was the fact that label directions were sometimes printed in languages foreign to the market areas. Further, it was charged that mothers adopting the formula could neither obtain pure water nor keep the artificial nipples sterilized. In addition, to save money mothers diluted the mix.

The battle pitted reputable public groups such as the National Council of Churches against staid food producers such as the Swiss firm, Nestle S.A. Concerned health, business, and management professionals were involved on both sides, as well as at the United Nations, which ultimately became the arena for the long-lingering battle. Out of this experience one company in particular, Ross Laboratories, made several changes in marketing procedures and set up a special task force to study Third World concerns (See Nickel, 1980). This is the sort of positive action now being taken by many multinationals through their corporate relations programs; the pattern could well be adopted by other corporations as well as by professional organizations. It is difficult to understand how large organizations or involved professionals could avoid dealing with such issues in ways appropriate to their practices without appearing uncaring.

ENERGY

Considerations of population, nutrition, and health lead to that of energy. Growing populations require increasing amounts of it, especially if per-capita consumption increases in order to provide increased productivity, health services, and generally higher material wealth.

Modern civilization is built on the utilization of energy to drive machines and to supplement and enhance muscle power. In the coal era and even more in the brief petroleum era, the abundance and transportability of fuel made possible an enormous flowering of cities, with cheap lighting, heating, and transportation. Society came to take for granted annual increases in energy consumption and to regard them as natural, necessary, and desirable. As late as the early 1970s, no end was foreseen to increases in energy production deemed essential for continued economic growth.

Suddenly the great debate over energy was ignited by the Arab Oil Boycott of 1973. Not only did Americans realize with a shock that their supplies of petroleum could be interrupted by other countries, but also that relatively finite supplies of petroleum would be exhausted in the foreseeable future, given present patterns of annual increases in consumption. Americans also learned that about 40 percent of the world's energy was consumed by their nine percent of the world population.

Two positions emerged in the public debate over energy. One continued to contend that increased production of energy was essential for growth and advocated the search for alternate sources. The other position held that the conservation of energy would provide a less polluting and saner response to the energy crisis domestically, as well as easing demand for scarce world supplies, freeing them for use by needy nations elsewhere.

An ethical analysis of the two positions would identify costs connected with both that will have to be borne by someone. Justice would argue that those who get the benefits of conservation (such as a cleaner environment) should share the costs (less money or work) or, alternatively, that those who increase their wealth from greater production should also bear the costs of more pollution. Unfortunately the relationship between costs and benefits has not worked out toward greater justice in the intervening years. The poorest nations on earth have suffered the most from increasing prices of petroleum. Some developing nations, such as Brazil, are able to turn with some success to alternate energy sources. But others go further into debt, squandering scarce foreign exchange on the highly expensive petroleum necessary to maintain their manufacturing and transportation processes. An omen of the future, perhaps, was seen in an incident in 1978 in which one entire nation of 10 million people temporarily ran out of gas due to such difficult financial problems that the country could not import crude oil for a time.

The debate over how best to resolve the energy problem continues unabated. Meanwhile, individuals and professions here and there find ways of contributing to the solution rather than to the problem. One profession in particular, as noted in Chapter 9, has made a response that deserves notice both for its own merits and as an example of ways in which professional organizations can respond to global issues. As the energy shortage deepened in the 1970s, the American Institute of Architects established an Energy Committee to help shape architecture's response to the energy shortage. That committee worked to revise the design protocols used in architectural practice so that new building designs would use half the energy or less than had been required with the earlier technology of the preceding period. This is an instance of professional action that will make a difference. In addition, one member of the Energy Committee heads a private architectural firm that refuses to execute a design for a client who will not include substantial energy conservation measures.

But while benefiting from successes in conservation and new sources of energy, American society still faces enormous problems. In the words of philosopher Alasdair MacIntyre (1979, p. 9):

> The debate about energy . . . will reveal to that society that it is . . . involved in a moral crisis as well as in an energy crisis. This prospect is a dismaying one and requires courage: We do not know how to reason together morally in an effective way. And this lack—just because it is something wanting in the social order as a whole—will never be remedied unless we face it as a society.

CONCLUSION

Our discussion has been merely illustrative, not exhaustive, of the sorts of ethical reflection that ought to be taking place in professional societies and in individual minds in a world struggling with survival issues. We have been able to deal with neither the full range of facts nor with the complexities and ambiguities of any of the situations explored. Nor have we mentioned other issues of even greater importance that cry out for solution: nuclear warfare and the arms race, the increasing reliance in our society on legal as opposed to moral restraints, the haphazard burgeoning of technology.

Even in this brief space, however, we have utilized elements of the framework for ethical decision making introduced in Chapter 3. That framework asks us to determine whether a situation has an ethical dimension of significance. Each of the problems discussed in the foregoing could be regarded as an economic, political, or cultural problem. But we discovered that each has a weighty ethical dimension as well, normally involving justice or fair dealing between nations or between corporations and consumers.

The framework also asks us to determine the facts relevant to a situation. The difficulty of adequately ascertaining the facts is pointed out by the discovery that, in many situations, experts differ among themselves as to which facts are important or what the facts are. Further, from the brief history of the energy problem we learn that the relevant facts change as situations develop. Thus, one must recognize the difficulty of achieving an adequate factual appraisal when doing ethical reflection. But the difficulty does not absolve one of the obligation to examine the factual dimensions as well as one can. Ethics is the art of *informed* judgment.

The same framework for decision making asks us to inquire how one's general vision of life's purposes bears on the situation in question. Those guided by hedonistic philosophies, that is, by visions of life in which one's own pleasure is paramount, will scrutinize each situation guided by the standard of self-interest. Utilitarians will be guided by the standard of the greatest good for the greatest number. Deontologists will apply some general principle such as justice. Persons committed to a covenantal worldview such as that introduced in Chapter 9 will seek to fathom the intentions of God in each historical situation and determine one's responsibility to neighbor in that light.

These observations lead us to a conclusion about the value of the framework for ethical decision making. By noting how each of the major worldviews would lead to a different assessment of the energy, food and nutrition, and population problems, it becomes clear that the framework in itself does not lead to uniform conclusions. The framework is an empty form. The values and worldviews with which one fills that form will be decisive in guiding ethical reflection and shaping judgment. The value of the framework is to help persons bring an orderly procedure into ethical reflection.

It is at this point, when one recognizes the differences implied in the varieties of ethics, the contrasts between different worldviews, and the uncertainties necessitated by the difficulty of determining the facts about a situation, that the importance of good character comes to the fore again. Though good character in itself does not guarantee a valid appraisal of facts, it does motivate one to pursue diligently the relevant facts and inclines one against unscrupulous biasing of the picture. Character gives one the courage to continue through the framework to the actual making of a decision and the adopting of a strategy for action while recognizing the need for continuing review and evaluation. So while character in itself is no substitute for systematic reflection in ethical decision making, it seems to be a necessary condition for doing well at it.

Overall, the inquiring professional mind does not rest until it examines the moral dimensions of trends in the world at large. It is on the canvas of world history that the responsibility of the professions to the quality and the continuing viability of human life will ultimately be tested.

References and Suggestions for Further Reading

Brown, Lester R. 1974. *By Bread Alone*. New York: Praeger. Policy study on food supply and population.

Center for Ethics and Social Policy. n.d. *Ethics for a Crowded World: A Seminar Series*. Berkeley: Graduate Theological Union. Factual background and ethical reflection on 10 global issues.

Dyck, Arthur J. 1980. "Triage and Charity in Population Policy," *National Forum*, Spring, pp. 36-38. Arguments against "life-boat ethics."

Goulet, Denis. 1974. *A New Moral Order: Studies in Development Ethics and Liberation Theology*. Maryknoll: Orbis Books.

MacIntyre, Alasdair. 1979. "Power Industry Morality," *Symposium: Science, Technology and the Human Prospect* (advertising supplement to the *New York Review of Books*), pp. 7-9.

Mesarovic, Mihajlo D. and E. Pestel. 1974. *Mankind at the Turning Point*. London: Hutchinson. Deals systematically with economic history, food supply, population, and power resources.

Nickel, Herman. 1980. "The Corporation Haters," *Fortune*, June 16. Unfortunately biased report on corporate critics and how business might learn from them and deal with them.

Stivers, Robert L. 1976. *The Sustainable Society: Ethics and Economic Growth*. Philadelphia: Westminster Press. An ecumenical approach.

Stobaugh, R. and Daniel Yergin. 1979. *Energy Future: Report of the Energy Project at the Harvard School of Business*. New York: Random House.

Think More About It

1. Is the professional organization with which you are identified seeking systematically to address any of the great global questions of our time? If not, what set of factors would be necessary for it to become willing to do so?

2. Can you think of one example of a professional person who has devoted himself or herself to addressing one of the great global questions and has made a difference? What personal characteristics account for this person's involvement and success? What strategies or plans for action did he or she follow?

3. What suggestions would you make for the benefit of professionals who are dealing with clients whose cultural outlooks are quite different than those of the professionals? Who should adjust to whom, and how? For example, think of a scientifically trained health professional practicing in a traditional, nonliterate population.

4. If a professional is retained by a client whose wishes for the project run contrary to the professional's commitments to long-term health or environmental standards, how should the professional respond? Think, for example, of a chemical engineer designing a process for a firm that wishes to dump resulting toxic wastes in a hazardous manner in order to save money.

ELEVEN

A Future for Professional Ethics

An era of continuously increasing social scale entailing substantial changes in the professions and professional ethics seems to be upon us. If we have done our historical and sociological work carefully enough, striking changes are already upon us. Let's summarize our conclusions about three important changes that we have previously identified.

PLURALISM AND THE FUTURE OF PROFESSIONAL ETHICS

Perhaps the most important background change for the future of professional ethics is the increase in scale of society, which means more people in ever-denser interactions over larger areas. One crucial aspect of the increase in scale is the growing dominance of large organizations. Each profession must discover how to better adapt to bureaucracy without losing the distinctive features of professionalism. Until very recently the rules and procedures of most professions have been built on the assumption of individuals working in private practice or in small-scale settings such as three- or four-person partnerships. But the solo practitioner is becoming a rarity in most fields and less prevalent even in medicine and law, the last holdouts against bureaucratization among the professions. Adaptations to confront the ethical challenges of large-scale organizations are evident in, for example, some engineering societies' provisions for support of members who suffer losses due to resisting unethical practices in their employing organizations. But these adjustments are probably mere clues to greater changes to come as each profession seeks to maintain professional standards and ideals under these new and challenging circumstances.

What are the challenges that increase of scale brings to the ethics of the professions? Each major type of ethics helps us to see the picture differently, just as each tool helps the carpenter accomplish a different task. The utilitarian criterion of the greatest good for the greatest number would lead one to think approvingly of increasingly inclusive networks of human interaction as greater numbers tied together over larger areas would probably increase the amount of good, whether pleasure or utility, available to each. However, the commitment to safeguarding individual freedoms would lead to concern over threats to personal and professional freedom and autonomy through bureaucratic control and regulation.

Different observations would be made by a deontologist, one concerned for obeying the principle of justice, for example. A question for professional ethics would be whether the professional services being rendered are fairly distributed rather than unfairly directed to privileged classes. For instance, does our mixed medical insurance system of private and public insurers adequately and fairly care for the needs of all? Such a standard would compel one to do one's best to make certain that justice is being creatively pursued, or at least that injustices are not perpetrated in large-scale institutions.

Still other questions would be raised by a person committed to an ethic of concern for persons and communities. While sharing a concern for justice and freedom, this personalist-professional would probably also feel obligated to raise serious questions about the regard of professions for the autonomy of clients. Certainly, the seeming dehumanization of persons through reducing full humanity to computer-compatible sets of statistics would be a high priority issue. The personalist-professional would seek to shape the process of change so as to safeguard the personal qualities of clients and of all the practitioners involved and to promote centers of loving concern within the larger framework of large-scale organizations.

These brief sketches reconfirm a point that has been made before: the moral judgments made about a situation by one person may differ from those made by another, resulting from dissimilar questions raised and perspectives applied. This has always been true; it is a fact of logic. However, it has not always been evident before our era of vast social scale, since localist societies normally have been limited to singular, common ethical traditions. Large-scale society forces the issue of pluralism; the reality of varied ethical commitments must be faced and dealt with.

To put ethical pluralism into perspective, two comments must be made. The first is to observe that despite pluralism, society seems to cohere and to make necessary adjustments. This is probably explainable by the fact that, in practice, ethics is not a simple, mechanical deduction from certain premises but is, instead, the result of personal discretion and wisdom. Ethics is an art. Once this is recognized, one may regard moral judgments as presumptions or first approximations, open to change as time passes and as one experiences and reflects more, or to revision as new perspectives are reached in the give-and-take of debate. Although one may take absolutist positions with very good reason in extreme circumstances, normally a person is willing to learn from and to contribute to others of sound reason and good will. The result is normally a public consensus that enables decision making despite the continued pluralism of outlooks. Once this is recognized, room exists between professionals of different moral persuasions for discussion, persuasion, and growth of outlook.

The second comment, however, is that creative use of different moral persuasions, rather than mere tolerance of them, is of great importance for modern professions. We need perspectives and procedures designed to bring out the best in each position, rather than to plummet each to the lowest-common-denominator accommodation, in order to arrive at creative moral consensuses. *A creative moral consensus is a shared judgment among good-willed and reasonable people about the moral qualities of a situation that moves each party toward deeper insight rather than she or he would have attained individually.* One of the challenges to professions and to societies in the modern era is to become much more skilled in the creative use of ethical pluralism.

Of course, a certain consensus might be destructive, not creative, and perhaps especially if based on egoism. One must raise questions about every consensus, test it, and reject or support it, including the broad consensus that exists in our society. The observation has been pressed upon us many times that egoism is a growing factor in the ethics of the professions and seems to be challenging or even displacing the more traditional enablement ethics. One might, with sound reasons, assert that the emerging "moral" consensus in our society is based largely on egoism. In keeping with the need to question each significant consensus, this one should be tested also.

First, though, let us review some of the reasons that have come to light for thinking that the factor of egoism is an increasingly dominant one. A proponent of egoism would judge the value of increasing social scale and technology from the standpoint of: what's in it for me? Professionals, professional organizations, and bureaucracies in which professionals are highly represented would probably view the increasing scale as a good trend in general, because it would seem to give them greater scope for the sale of their services and for raising the prices they charge while loosening the bonds of accountability that personal knowledge of practitioners by clients and customers seems to impose. But the growth of regulation of business and professions, another concomitant of the increase of scale, would be counted as a cost, or perhaps as an evil, since it acts to restrain unimpeded free choice in the pursuit of self-interest. This line of thought is quite close to what one actually reads in the platforms of both major political parties, sees in the annual reports of many corporations, and hears in the conversation of professional friends. Hence, if we have read the signs carefully enough, there are grounds for thinking that a consensus is, in fact, emerging around the self-interest ethic of egoism.

Other ethical systems would find cause for alarm in the dominance of egoism. A utilitarian would point out that it ignores the overriding issue, the common good. A situationist of the school of Joseph Fletcher would fault it for flouting the principle of love by trying to corner the good things of life for one's self rather than to distribute them fairly. A personalist would condemn the egoist consensus for using other persons, whether one's clients or others, as simply the means to advance one's own ends. No other major perspective in ethics would be pleased with the dominance of egoism and the consensus forming around it.

So far as egoism is concerned, each profession has its own story to tell. The ethic of egoism may exert a much stronger grip on the ethos or culture of one profession than on that of another. But whatever egoism's strength in a particular profession may be, it is important to recognize that it is quite alien to the indigenous professional moral theme of enablement. It threatens the very notion of a profession because it shifts the meaning from that of a collegial body bound together for service to that of an expedient band of conspirators organized to serve themselves at the expense of others. Trust between colleagues is endangered and the relationship with clients, government, and the world shifts from cooperation to aggression. The groundwork is laid for a story very different from that of the past, and the fears of those critics quoted in Chapter 2 who see the professions as vehicles of class dominance seem to be justified.

If the ethic of egoism were to consolidate its grip, it is doubtful that professions as we have known them could endure. Regulation would increase as the public discovered its increasing need for protection against professional exploitation and abuse. The autonomy of the profession would be forfeited, and it would assume the nature of an instrument for economic competition. The profession as a servant body trusted by clients and the public would disappear. Egoism, dominant at last, would throw the last spadeful of dirt on the grave of the professions.

If it is desirable to continue with the moral commitment to enablement, professionals will need to face up to the crisis stemming from the rise of egoism in our culture. Egoism is not a suitable solution to the problems posed by. pluralism. Rank-and-file professionals, as well as their leaders, will have to decide to fight this increasing stock placed in egoism and to promote some form of enablement instead. Otherwise, continuity with the older orientation of the professions will be lost.

RELIGION AND THE FUTURE OF PROFESSIONAL ETHICS

So far we have concluded that professions need to deal creatively with the consequences of increasing social scale. They need to work creatively with the situation of ethical pluralism while finding a way to discourage the growth of egoism. They need to discover a framework for a broad, participatory ethic of enablement. It is fitting at this point to test the covenantal religious perspective to determine whether it meets these requirements, and we shall do it here.

The contributions of other disciplines have to be recognized first in order to put those of religion in a proper perspective. We have learned that professional ethics, from the standpoint of the current divisions of learning, is an interdisciplinary effort in which the social sciences, philosophy, and religion all contribute. Specifically, the social sciences provide the best techniques for gathering the empirical data necessary for ethical reflection and strategy building, while philosophy bequeaths the clearest formulations of the various types of ethics. One who wishes to do professional ethics needs acquaintance with the social sciences and philosophy and to appreciate their contributions.

What, then, can a religious outlook reasonably be expected to contribute to professional ethics? We have already indicated that both deontological and teleological ethics, the ethics of obligation and of aspiration, can be found embodied in the teachings of most religions. Hence, religion does not seem to prescribe any additional or particularly unique type of ethics. But what religion, at least the benevolent sort, can add to professional ethics is a new spirit by supplying a context (a covenant, a worldview) and a center (a calling) as a framework supportive of moral reflection in a pluralistic setting. Such a religious framework promotes openness and cooperation among adherents of various points of view by emphasizing commonalities.

Covenant suggests that the professional participates with others in bonds of shared values and mutual obligations. The community is one of enablement by its nature—enablement of clients, peers, and society at large as well as of one's own development. The covenant of the profession is embedded in more inclusive covenants culminating in that of the human community itself, and it enfolds less inclusive covenants such as those of service teams of workers in a particular setting. Finally, each covenant, including the professional one, includes a vertical dimension that points to a providential factor beyond human limitations and which participates in our lives and makes them possible. In short, covenantal thinking provides a comprehensive worldview, a framework for professional ethics.

Being primarily a creature of the West coast, my life brings me daily into contact with Jews, Buddhists, and members of other religions. More and more, it becomes clear that such religious pluralism is the wave of the future, as circles of interaction enlarge and both peoples and ideas migrate back and forth across the world. Hence it is important to find a religious framework that allows Christians to participate with professionals of other religious outlooks. The concept of *covenant* seems to allow such cooperation without placing any one religious tradition in a superordinate position. For the Christian the concept of the covenant has deep biblical roots in the life of Jesus as well as in God's agreements with Israel and with Abraham and Adam. The covenantal idea informs the Jew as well as the Muslim, since they share in the same stream of faith as the Christian. But many other religions have their own indigenous notions of covenant. It is found at the heart of African and native American religions and is suggested by the concept of brotherhood *(sangha)* in Buddhism and by caste location in Hinduism. *Covenant* seems to be a deep, fundamental reality of the common human heritage which has roots in each particular tradition. Therefore it has the potential of forming the contextual framework for cooperation among peoples of all religious outlooks. Equally important, an implied covenant of trust can appeal to compassionate secular humanists as well, although they would reject the vertical dimension.

The other concept, *calling*, presupposes the covenant. Within the covenant God reveals a purpose of calling for human life. In classical Christian terms the purpose is to serve the glory of God and the welfare of fellow human beings, but this can be translated into our terminology by saying that each professional person and organization is to work for a higher quality of life in professional relationships, all the way from that with the individual client to those involving broad social issues. The *calling* also establishes professions as one among other kinds of human work, since all people share in the same general calling. The meaning of the professions is based primarily on the fact that all constructive work is valued by God.

Like that of the *covenant*, the concept of *calling* is religious, but neither narrowly nor exclusively so. First, the religious history of the concept is widespread and encompasses Islam, Judaism, and Christianity. Second, traditions other than those named have their own concepts of the purpose of life, so that Buddhists and others could probably agree with little hesitation to the ethical implications of the idea of the calling. Agnostics would have trouble only in externalizing the source of the calling in a providential factor, but might well accept the ethical thrust. Thus once again, as with covenant, the concept of calling sketched here can hardly be called exclusivist, and persons who adhere to it ought to be able to develop positive working relationships with all people of good will who work for increased quality of life.

Within the moral commitments of each profession are the individual commitments of each professional. Each is unique to the individual that holds it. What a religious commitment can do for a professional is to provide a way of centering one's own moral commitment in yet another, grander story that makes a life of enablement possible. The Jew, for instance, would find a center in the story of the Exodus, in which God saves the wandering people and calls them to be a light to all the nations. Through this people the nations are to be blessed. The individual Jew is to be a vehicle of this blessing by demonstrating God's loving concern in all aspects of life, including work. Every informed Jew knows this story; it centers life in a history of divine enablement.

The Buddhist also possesses a story, recalling the rich young prince who forsook the wealth of the palace for material poverty and religious enlightenment. Above all, this enlightened one, the Buddha, served suffering humanity. Instead of immediately entering the state of release from his own suffering, he tarried to show others the way. The kindness and love of the Buddha strengthen one by demonstrating that life centers in love for all creatures.

For the Christian, the story centers in a person, Jesus, who healed the sick, fed the hungry, and taught those who would hear the words of life. Jesus provides a center for the professional by demonstrating a pattern of self-giving love. The victorious resurrection, following the humiliating death by crucifixion, vouches for the superiority of the self-giving life in the ultimate scale of history. This story calls the Christian professional to a life of enablement and, like others mentioned here, precludes an ethic of egoism.

Just as the concepts of covenant and calling seem to pass the test of religious pluralism, so important in our world of increasing social scale, so they seem to pass the test of ethical pluralism as well. They provide an open religious worldview that can be related meaningfully and supportively to an ethic of obligation, such as a moral law theory, or to an ethic of aspiration, such as utilitarianism. Neither the covenant nor the calling seems to dictate any particular ethical system among the formal types we have surveyed. What these concepts do, however, is to provide a framework and a center that shifts the perspective of any ethic away from the strictly human and toward an ultimate meaning tinged with mystery. This framework and center underscore the vaster scale, the longer time frame, the larger whole that justifies each of our smaller visions of the good life. Religion transforms professional ethics through a telescopic expansion of the meaning of all that is good in each of them.

In summary, a religious outlook of the sort suggested here does provide help for grappling creatively with the challenges that come from vast social scale and pluralism. This sort of outlook encourages a healthy openness to religious and ethical pluralism while encouraging each specific tradition to act at its best and highest levels of insight. It supports the moral theme of enablement that lies at the heart of professional ethics. If an egoistic ethic is useless or even destructive when tested by the criteria suggested in this study, the perspectives inculcated by covenant and calling do not fail, even though we may often fail them.

A PATH TOWARD THE FUTURE

How can a professional, or a lay person for that matter, place confidence in these religious concepts of calling and covenant in a sci-tech era? One of the conclusions toward which the ideas in this study lead is that if modern life has called naive religion into question, the premises of modern life itself, including those of rationalism which underlie science and technology, are questionable also and not as solid as they were once perceived to be. The premises of modern life have led to depersonalization and egoism, which are dead ends so far as professional life, long-term, is concerned. Some third approach seems needed as an opening toward the future.

The direction needed at this juncture in the history of professional ethics is neither to react to naive faith nor to become fixated on modernity, but to press beyond each of these older patterns. What a faith on the other side of modernity would mean is the recognition of the limits of science with acknowledgement of its merits and benefits. The role of a faith in forming a total outlook on life would be acknowledged, while the role of reason would be affirmed as well. Finally, the meaning of the old religious symbols, such as the Exodus and the cross, so essential to a conventional worldview, would be recovered.

Not many have traveled this path. Not the professional associations, to be sure, which seem to have become preoccupied with modernity, and probably not more than a few professionals. Some trail breaking has been done, however. For instance, one sociologist has probed for a postmodern religious faith and has conveyed his experiences in a series of writings. What he claims to have discovered is that within our own human experience are to be found the "signals of transcendence" (Berger, 1970, p. 52). And, since the professions are part of human experience, those signals are undoubtedly present in one's professional practice.

The path we are advocating is quite different from the recent and seemingly fashionable attempts, popularized by the Moral Majority, to reimpose a fundamentalist Christian perspective on our pluralistic society. Whether backed with erudition, as in the case of Francis Schaeffer (1977), or filled with sheer rant, as with Tim LaHaye (1980), this approach grossly oversimplifies our morally complex society by dividing it into just two competing ways of life: Christian and humanist. All social ills are identified with humanism, the scapegoat, and contrasted to the unquestioned benefits to be derived from an exclusively Christian interpretation. Furthermore, it is assumed that "Christian" means fundamentalist, in which one reads directly from ancient Old Testament and New Testament texts to contemporary professional and social situations. Such an approach is as unfair to Christianity as it is to other religions and to humanism, and I wish to dissociate very clearly the present proposal from that one.

In the present proposal, the acknowledged need of regrounding professional life in religious vision is met by calling for professionals to be sensitive to moments of religious experience, "signals of transcendence," in the very practice of their professions. What "signals of transcendence" might professionals expect to find? Such signals might include, by way of example, the inner strength and joy of a patient—even a dying one—that seems to fly in the face of all circumstances. Or the need of the professional team to plumb resources beyond those of rational analysis in settling a difficult problem encountered in practice. Any experience that points beyond the limits of professional life to more ultimate dimensions of wisdom and power should be explored as a possible signal of transcendence.

The moral danger that comes in ignoring the transcendent in professional life was pinpointed accurately by Leon Jaworski (1976, p. 278) after reflecting on his experience as a Watergate prosecutor. Jaworski said, "The tapes! The teachings of right and wrong were forgotten in the White House. Little evils were permitted to grow into great evils, small sins escalated into big sins." As Jaworski continued, he linked this moral failure directly to a religious failure:

> In the hours and hours of tape-recorded conversations to which I listened, not once was there a reference to the Glory of God, not once a reference to seeking spiritual guidance through prayer. Our Lord was mentioned, yes, but on each pitiable occasion his name was taken in vain. If only there had been an occasional prayer for help, an occasional show of compassion! Why was there not just a simple statement such as: "May we hold our honor sacred. . . . " How different might have been the course of government if there had been an acknowledgement of God as the source of right instead of a denial of Him in a seemingly unending series of ruthless actions.

In contrast to a studied denial of God, when the path of religious sensitivity is followed, the old symbols will take on new life. The talk of a religious dimension to ethical practice will no longer seem artificial, but will rather come to be regarded as integral and essential to the professional way of life. The basis for the reconstruction of professional ethics will have been laid. A note of realism is needed: exploitation will never be rooted out entirely. But the balance can be redressed in favor of enablement. The foundations will have been laid for a century of professional pursuit of a higher quality of life for all creatures.

References and Suggestions for Further Reading

Berger, Peter. 1970. *A Rumor of Angels*. Garden City, N.Y.: Doubleday and Co., Inc.

LaHaye, Tim. 1980. *Battle for the Mind*. Old Tappan, N.J.: Fleming-Revell. A frightening scenario for imposing the imperial reign of religious fundamentalism on American life.

Jaworski, Leon. 1976. *The Right and the Power*. New York: Reader's Digest Press; Houston: Gulf Publishing Company.

McCoy, Charles S. 1980. *When Gods Change: Hope for Theology*. Nashville: Abingdon. A creative statement of covenantal theology for an era of global culture and religious pluralism.

Schaeffer, Francis and C. Everett Koop. 1977. *Whatever Happened to the Human Race?* Old Tappan, N.J.: Fleming-Revell. A protest by two erudite scholars against the dominance of secular humanism but for the establishment of religious fundamentalism as the law of the land.

Walton, Clarence C. 1980. "Business Ethics: The Present and the Future." *Hastings Center Report* 10 (5): pp. 16-20. A review of recent literature.

Think More About It

1. Can you give an example of a professional whose religious commitment seems to support a relationship of client enablement and an attitude of openness to others of different ethical persuasion?

2. What are the possible relationships between your own religious worldview and science? Do they compete with each other? Are they harmonious? Explain your present understanding.

3. In what ways might a person in your chosen profession experience "signals of transcendence" right in the midst of the work-life?

Index